PROSPERITY CONSCIOUSNESS

Books by Audrey Craft Davis

Metaphysical Techniques That Really Work
Making Love with God
Prosperity Consciousness
Metaphysical Encounters of a Fourth Kind

"The good I do is the rent that I pay
for the space I occupy on this planet."

PROSPERITY CONSCIOUSNESS

A Metaphysical Guide to Your Natural Wealth

Audrey Craft Davis,
Ms.D., Ps.D., D.D.

Blue Dolphin Publishing

Published by Blue Dolphin Publishing, Inc.
P.O. Box 8, Nevada City, CA 95959
Orders: 1-800-643-0765
Web: www.bluedolphinpublishing.com

ISBN: 978-1-57733-203-9

Library of Congress Cataloging-in-Publication Data

Davis, Audrey Craft.
   Prosperity consciousness : a metaphysical guide to your natural
wealth / Audrey Craft Davis.
        p. cm.
   ISBN-13: 978-1-57733-203-9 (pbk. : alk. paper)
   1. Wealth—Religious aspects.   2. Finance, Personal—
Miscellanea.   I. Title.

   BL65.W42D38 2006
   131—dc22
                                        2006029543

Cover design by James Craft.

Printed in the United States of America

10   9   8   7   6   5   4   3   2   1

Dedication

As with all my books, I dedicate this one to my wonderful late companion and husband, Lou, whose compassion, assistance and understanding, made writing this book and life itself, a "Magnificent Journey." To my Angels and my daughter, Alice Schuler, my son, James V. Craft, my sister, Minnie Beam, and the members of my family who have gone on: my mother and father, sisters, Lorainne, Kathryn and Helen and my late brother, Jim, who still inspire me.

Contents

Preface

In my counseling, one of the biggest problems I find is a definite need to get out of poverty thinking and into prosperity consciousness. Once people learn to change the things that are blocking their path to evolvement, they become self-assured individuals. Then, prosperity is free to flow to them. When money is no longer the main issue of their life, they are free to develop their talents, give back to the world and be of assistance to those who are still struggling. This is why we are here: to help our fellow man.

CHAPTER ONE

It Is Natural to Be Wealthy

"Whatever you vividly imagine, ardently desire, sincerely believe and enthusiastically act upon must inevitably happen,"
—Paul J. Myers of the SMI Institute

Magnificent Journey follows this formula. It is about manifesting wealth. As I became enthralled with the ideas streaming through my mind, it was as though an angel appeared. Then I remembered when I asked my spirit guide (my angel) how I would know when he was near; he said to put my attention at my right shoulder. As I did, the subject matter began to take shape and I knew the book was underway.

It is costly to be poor and it serves no purpose. As a matter of fact it is easier to manifest wealth than to give in to poverty. All the prophets and main characters of the Bible were wealthy. They owned "much land and many cattle," the scripture says. If any one of them lacked anything, the first question was imminent, "Wherein have you sinned?" It is obvious that God's people were intended to be wealthy.

How can we help others or the planet if we ourselves are living in poverty? We live in a rich universe and God has many

1

ways of caring for it and us. Here is a good example. Why was it snowing in areas where it almost never snowed before? The angels were energizing the snow flakes to purify the atmosphere.

The impurities were magnetized into the snow flakes which then soaked into the earth. Then the angels multiplied and energized the earth worm population to eat and aerate the garbage and soil to transmute the pollution. This adds moisture to the soil which in turn creates more nutritious organic food. The result: many new businesses, earth worm, compost, and organic farming. When we get in tune with our universe, we realize God is in charge. We don't need to get uptight about anything.

Do you know that God has his angels to harvest all the lovely thoughts, words and deeds in the universe? Then they distribute them all over the planet to offset the negative, harmful thoughts and deeds which cause the black energy. We need to be co-creators in this endeavor by using every opportunity to change darkness into light. Even the scientists know we need more light in this universe. They have been trying to invent an instrument whereby they can extract light from deep space. It would seem that it would be obvious—man must do this with his mind.

Wealth can easily come about after we achieve prosperity consciousness, which allows us to see money and wealth for what it is—energy. To get what we want, there must be a transfer of this energy. When you become so in tune with money that you do not know if you have any in your possession, at present, you have the correct consciousness for wealth.

There was a time when I felt I had to carry a hundred dollar bill in my purse at all times to remind me of abundance. I have grown out of that, thank God. Millionaires seldom carry money. They know money is energy, a medium of exchange.

Wealth is so much more than money. It is money, of course, but prosperity consciousness is "a knowing" that God created a rich universe and supplied it with everything we should ever need. It is also the realization that, to have what you want, takes from no one. We must want wealth for others as well as for ourselves.

Oh, man has exploited the wealth, but that was never God's intention. If greed did not exist in our world, there would be enough of everything so that no one would ever go without. There are enough trees in Russia alone, to build a very substantial house for every man, woman and child on planet earth. Our technology is increasing to where there will soon be a cure for every disease known to man.

In my book *Metaphysical Techniques That Really Work* in the chapter entitled, "Is It My Right to Prosper," I assert that it is not a vice to be rich nor a virtue to be poor. I tell the reader that prosperity and abundance is our birthright. But you must not block your own progress by the way you think. I have made it a rule that if I don't want something to happen, I will refuse to think about it. Do you know that if you worry about a person or a situation, you bind that person or situation with whatever you are worried about.

Scripture tells us that we can bind things on earth and we can loose things on earth. First and foremost, if you feel life has been unfair, you must rid yourself of all thoughts of remorse, of being cheated, and ideas about how to get even. You need to count your loss as seed sown to the Universe.

Instead of dwelling on your loss, sow seeds (thoughts) of what you intend that harvest to bring forth. God looks at the intent. He doesn't look at the outward appearance, but rather, the heart. Seed must produce after its own kind. The Universal Law states, "Whatsoever you sow, that shall you also reap." You cannot change that law. This is why you must get rid of all adverse thoughts and feelings concerning money and riches. We must not sow that kind of seed. Most of us were taught not to expect a reward for the good that we do. This is in error of the law.

We definitely should expect a reward for every good thing we have ever done. We do not do it for this reason, but it is the law and we cannot change it. The magic word here is "expect." This is another way to say "faith." When teaching this subject, I ask the student to make a list of his or her good deeds and to realize they should be reaping a harvest from each and every one of them.

Often a student will ask, "What about the bad things I have done?" The scripture tells us that our Heavenly Father has cast these as far from us as the east is from the west, to be remembered no more. He knows that we, as human beings, are still in the learning process. Like any good parent, God makes allowances for our error consciousness. If God does not remember them and you do, you are trying to make yourself bigger than God, and you are not. Ask God to forgive you. Forgive yourself and move on!

Also, think of the times you have made a bad business venture, or you failed at something. Perhaps someone owes you and refuses to repay the debt. Release all feelings of remorse to the Universe. And since nature abhors a vacuum, you must fill that space. Anytime you rid yourself of anything, fill that empty space with a white light. Then, fill your mind with visions of a harvest that is awaiting your reaping the good you have done.

As you do this, you will have helped yourself, and you will have also changed the lives of others by turning darkness into light, as you will see in the following chapter. Why have you not been paid for the good you have done? The reason is, because you did not know to expect a return. Expectancy is faith.

But now that you know, you have an avalanche of good awaiting your reaping. If you lose money, or experience failure in some other way, realize this is another deposit to the Universe. I have seen this work miraculously in my own life and in the lives of many others, but only after they began "expecting" to receive.

The following affirmation is very effective: "I claim my good of past and present. I accept my blessings. I deserve and I welcome them. My good is at hand and I experience it, now."

End with seeing a rich harvest. See it NOW! Plan what you will do with the wealth and who you will want to share it with. Do this morning and night. Then let it go until next time.

If you keep thinking of it, your little conscious mind will try to interfere. It will show you how this is not logical, how it cannot happen, for this is the way our conscious mind works. It can never deal with the supernatural. Keep in mind that your conscious mind is only five percent of your total mind power.

I advise you to tithe. In doing so, you declare God as your partner. And He only asks for ten percent. Most partners would demand half. But give only the amount that you can give with joy. It does no good to give begrudgingly. You can also tithe your time, talents and thoughts if you can do it joyfully.

I teach my students to treasure-map. If you have never experienced treasure-mapping, try it. It is the most powerful prayer you can pray and it works like magic. Why do I say it is a prayer? If you ask God for something, you must see a picture of what you want. You cannot think without seeing a picture. In treasure-mapping, you post the actual picture of what you desire, in a book or on a poster, as well. This allows your logical conscious mind to come into play.

I use a photo album with a plastic cover for each sheet. That way when your picture has materialized, you can easily remove it and replace it with a picture of some other dream or goal. Here is the technique: Place a picture of the desired object on the page. Under the picture write: "This or something better. Thank you, Father," then sign your name. When you sign your name, be aware that it is now a contract. Do this on each page.

When you think a thought, it is powerful; when you speak it, it has more power, and when you write it, it becomes a contract.

Why write, "This or something better?" Because your idea of thinking big, might be to ask for a Cadillac, but God may want you to have a Lear jet. You always get more than you ask for. Your next question is possibly, "How fast can it happen?"

I would answer you with a question, "How much can you believe or how big is your faith?"

I have seen miracles many times as a result of treasure-mapping, like having a new car materialize overnight to someone who has no money and no credit.

I have had people ask if it is all right to treasure-map to win the lottery. I say, "Why pin God down to one means of getting you the money you want? He owns the whole Universe. Ask for the money (as much as you can believe), but don't tell God where it must come from."

The chapter "My Cosmic Bank Account" shows you another means of becoming wealthy. I say, "Why not play all your cards. If the harvest is too large, surely you can find someone with whom you would like to share your fortune."

The following is my own true revelation. I know this idea came from my angels.

CHAPTER TWO

My Cosmic Bank Account

It all started when God had a great lesson for me. You know, one of those times when we think our world is falling apart.

But God can come through our desperation and bring us tremendous awards from what seems like pure and simple devastation, if we can believe. Haven't you found that some of the greatest blessings of your life came from what, at the time, seemed like the worst possible disaster?

It seems like sheer idiocy to say, "Thank God I lost that $200,000." But even as I say this, I know there is nothing lost in the kingdom. When we take our position as citizens of His Invisible Kingdom, as the Master taught, all power is ours.

I'll admit that for a time I had to fight everything in me to keep from crying out, "This is unfair. I worked hard for that money. God, why would you let this happen to me?" But as a citizen of the Invisible Kingdom, I released it all to the Universe. I declared, "I will count this money as seed which I sow as a deposit in my Cosmic Bank Account."

The money was earned from a business venture. Since it had been lost by what seemed like unjust action, I decided to invest it in something really sound. So I opened my Cosmic Bank Account.

I would never have spent that $200,000. One does not sell the goose that is laying the golden egg.

But rather, I would have enjoyed the dividends. If the $200,000 is not vested in my business, what better thing to earn dividends than a solid investment. I sowed it to the Universe in my very own Cosmic Bank Account.

So, since then, if I seem to have lost anything, or someone refused to pay back a loan, or if it seems I was cheated, or even if I honestly made a bad investment, I can't wait until I can get it deposited in my Cosmic Bank Account. Wow, another deposit!

You might ask, "Does it always work?" Well, this all happened over twenty years ago and I can honestly say that since then I have not wanted for anything I did not get, which includes seventy cruises and many trips around the world. I know that my good is at hand and I can have whatever I desire through the realization of my citizenship in the Invisible Kingdom of God—another way of saying, "I have attained true prosperity consciousness."

If we can get enough people to claim their right to this inner kingdom, we can change not only our world but the universe. Stop and think. If you owned a kingdom, would you ever need to ask or even give a thought to whether you could afford anything? You would know you can have anything your heart desires. Claim your citizenship, now.

I sent this article to a former teacher. He wrote me that the article saved his life. He had made a really bad investment and it had haunted him incessantly. He lay awake night after night, breaking out in a cold sweat, wondering how he could recover his loss or at least assuage his mind in some way.

He wrote, "Since reading your article, I released that (bad investment) and deposited it into my Cosmic Bank Account as you advised and I now sleep like a baby, knowing my good is at hand."

You should also deposit all the successes in your Cosmic Bank, as well. Recently, I advised a client to make a Cosmic Bank. I said, "It can be a tissue box, a jar or whatever you can make a slit through which you can slip a small piece of paper. Write on the container in large letters "My Cosmic Bank."

Then I instructed her to write on a slip of paper every good deed she could think of and deposit it into her Cosmic Bank.

I told her to start with the valuable books she had just sent me, and every time she did a good deed, to remember that it is a deposit. I went on to explain how wrong it was to have been taught that we should not expect anything for the good we do. That premise goes completely against cosmic law. "Whatsoever you sow, that you shall also reap," is the real law.

You do not do the good for that purpose, but if you do not expect something for the good you do, you are in error of the law.

I have had students tell me that they considered me the most generous person they knew. I replied, "Perhaps, but I do expect a reward from every good thing I do. That is not my motivation, but if I didn't expect a return, I would be a poor teacher."

Because you now know to expect to be paid for good you do, an avalanche of wealth could come showering down upon you at any moment! Expectation is another way of saying "faith." Jesus said, "As is your faith," another way to say, "Whatever you expect," "so be it unto you."

An excellent means of having lots of deposits is to ask God to let you be an instrument. Each day I pray, "Lord, make me and instrument. Where there is darkness, let me sow light; where there is doubt, faith; where there is despair, hope; where there is injury, pardon." As a result, I have many deposits for my account.

In class I often give this assignment: "Try to do a good deed without receiving a return." In every instance the student will come back to class with this typical reply, "It can't be done!"

Then they enumerate the blessings they received as a result of the good they have done. And the wonder of it all is, they always receive more than they sowed. Try it!

I have one more, small personal incident to share with you. But, I assure you it did not seem small at the time. I had rented my house and the occupant left it in a horrible condition. I spent $40,000 trying to make it livable. The grounds were atrocious.

I assigned the work on the lawn and driveway to a company owned by a woman who was down on her luck.

I knew better than to pay her in advance, but she kept telling me how she needed the money for her two small children. She even brought them over to show me. She may have borrowed them for all I know. She put in a few inexpensive shrubs and kept preying on my sympathy as to why she wasn't getting the work done.

After paying her, little by little, until she had an advance of $1500, I gave her an ultimatum: that she would get no more money until the work was caught up. Her next move was a real shocker, as she told me what a fool I had been.

She informed me that she was not coming back and was keeping my money. And furthermore, there was nothing I could do about it.

She moved back up north and she was right; there was not one thing I could do about it. Making a fool of me and boasting about it hurt more than losing the money. I wondered why God would stand by and let this thing happen to me when I was acting out of the goodness of my heart.

I'll have to admit that I lay awake, breaking out in a cold sweat, berating myself for being such a fool. But like the prodigal son, I finally came to my senses and realized that I have a rich Father who loves me and that I must get back to Him.

So, thank God I knew the way home. I deposited that loss of $1500 into my Cosmic Bank, knowing that the universe would repay me, for it all belongs to my very rich Father. Did He pay me back?

You bet I got paid! People even came to my door offering to do work for me at half the price I had planned to pay her.

My driveway and yard work was done at a fraction of her cost, and the man who did such a good job with my driveway offered to install me a new building. He even told me that he hated doing that kind of work, but he did it because he liked me. It got better and better. I saved far more than she had taken from me.

So deposit your good deeds into your Cosmic Bank account, along with every loss, even if you have made a bad investment or trusted someone you shouldn't have. You will get back far more than you sowed. We do reap what we sow. If you sow seeds of hurt, anger, of being cheated, any negative thought, word or deed—that is exactly what you will reap. God doesn't look at outward appearances, He looks at the heart—what you intended.

If we expect our reward from the people to whom we do the good, we have one source from which to reap. But if we turn it over to the Universe, which belongs to God, He has millions of different means of paying us back, and the harvest is always much, much more than we sow. Jesus said, "You might reap ten-fold, a hundred-fold, a thousand-fold or ten thousand-fold."

What makes the difference in the amount of return? The joy with which you sow. When you give with enthusiasm, your barns will overflow, your good will be heaped up and running over. He will pour you out a blessing so big you can't even contain it. You'll have to give some away and then it starts all over.

This is why I tell people to never give unless you can do it with joy. Happy giving works like fertilizer on a plant. You will have lots of deposits for your Cosmic Bank as you sow many wonderful seeds. But beware, you could become wealthy. Don't wait, claim your citizenship today and open your cosmic bank account!

I must share this story with you about one of my students. I asked her if she had made any recent deposits in her cosmic account. She shrugged her shoulders and admitted that she really hadn't. I said to her, "I can think of two very important deposits you should have made." She looked puzzled as I continued.

"Remember the day you told me about how your angels led you into purchasing things you would usually never buy for yourself? And what about the day you lay on my balance board as I counseled you?" That deposit should read, "Today I nurtured Helen."

She looked really perplexed. "But that was all for me!"

I reminded her, "Remember Jesus said, 'As you have done to any one of these my little ones, you have done unto me.' Helen, you are one of His little ones." So often we take care of everyone but ourselves.

In this next chapter, see how your every thought and word enters into the process; even your feelings count. It is not what happens to you that matters, it is the way you react to what happens; the way you feel about it makes the difference!

CHAPTER THREE

Your Thought Is a Command

Why is it that nothing can express in your life unless you give it permission? Because God put everything on this earth under man's dominion. How do you give that permission? By your thought or word. By thinking about it, you give it your very life force. It is your offspring and you are responsible for it. When you think of anything, it is the same as a command. It will materialize exactly as you see it.

It doesn't matter whether it is animal, idea, thing, matter or medicine. Try to think of any one of these and not see a picture. It is impossible. The picture in your mind is what gives the permission. It is analogous to angels. When we ask an angel to do something, they must do it, for God assigned them to us. Faith is another way of "commanding." When we believe something, we are commanding that thing to be exactly as we see it. With our thought we constantly mold the invisible into visible substance.

You might think of it this way. When a thought goes out into the ethers, a beautiful angel takes it and materializes it, for that angel knows its purpose is to fulfill your dreams. The angel goes by the picture in your mind. Even if it is a bad one, you sent it out there. So the angel has no authority to change that picture. The angel must materialize it just the way you sent it out!

Charles Fillmore, the founder of the Unity movement, tells us that our thoughts are so powerful they cause the very atoms of the universe to tremble and change place. Look at this example.

When Paul Crouch of TBN climbed upon the roof of the building he had just purchased, he saw (pictured in his mind) his TV station functioning perfectly in spite of the mountain that had blocked the former owner's signal for years. When he commanded the mountain to move and stop impeding the transmission of his TV station, it had no choice. When he said, "Mountain, I command you to move," for the first time the signal was clear. Paul's thought was a command. He took authority over the situation.

If we really knew how powerful our mind is, it would scare us to death. Do you know that there is enough power in one brain to run all the electricity for New York City for a year?

And if we wanted to make a map of one brain, it would take a sheet of paper the size of the state of Texas. You really have that kind of force within your mind.

Satan can do nothing unless he is allowed to come through the mind of man. Only man can give him permission. Satan is powerless unless man invites him in. I remember when Benny Hinn, the great healer and minister, did that very thing.

His ministry had become so powerful, he decided that he had better be prepared for anything. He decided to learn everything he could about demons just in case he might have an encounter with them. It is plain to see that Benny invited them in through his mind, by his thought. Guess what? Through Benny's mind, the demons came on the scene. God had to send Archangel Michael to fight them for Benny. He told how these demons attacked him and a huge angel came in and slammed the demons up against the wall and knocked them out.

He said that another angel came and told Archangel Michael that there was trouble in another place. So Archangel Michael told the other angel to take care of it ... that he had his hands full.

Satan has never been human. Only human beings were given dominion over all the earth. This is why Satan can only function through man. Satan can do nothing on his own. How unwittingly we give up our power, even as did the great Benny Hinn.

When a minister goes into the pulpit and teaches that Satan is the cause of all pain, illness and lack, does he realize he is giving Satan the power to inflict pain, illness and poverty?

The only way Satan or demons can get into our world is if we open the door. How do we do this? Through your thoughts and words.

You might say, "But what if the fearful thought just comes creeping out?" Jesus tells us we have an advocate with the Father.

The Father is flexible. There are many ways to use this advocate. One that I like was promulgated by the Masters of the Far East. Their premise is: If a wrong thought, feeling or word comes to mind, you are responsible for it since you gave it life.

It is your offspring so it is up to you to do something about it. Their advice: Say to that offspring, "I formed you imperfectly, so I send you back into the universe from which comes all things to be restructured. You cannot return to me except as love and light."

If that word or thought tries to reappear, say to it, "You do not exist. You have been restructured as light and love." For some, it might be enough to say, "Cancel" to that unwanted offspring. But to another, to just say "cancel" may seem like just a slap on the cheek.

If that word or thought persists, you may feel you need a club. If so, use the formula postulated by The Masters of the Far East.

You might ask why the picture in your mind did not work when that dog bit you or that thug robbed you? It did! It worked especially well. You changed the film (the picture). When confronted with the danger, your picture of confidence changed to one of fright.

Instead of seeing the dog stopping dead in his tracks when you commanded him, your picture changed to one of seeing the dog attacking you. And the thought of the thug did the same. You let your picture change from one of confidence to one of fear.

I heard the story of a man who believed that if he would say to any situation, "I behold the Christ in you," he would be protected. He got the opportunity to test his theory when a thug held him up in an alley, stuck a gun in his ribs and demanded his money. The man said to the robber, "I behold the Christ in you."

The thug again demanded his money swearing he was going to blow the man's head off if he did not comply. Again the man made the same declaration, as he pictured the robber having no power.

After making his demands several times and each time the man declared, "I behold the Christ in you," the gangster ran down the alley shouting over his shoulder, "You are crazy!"

Jesus said, "Know ye not that ye are gods?" Even if you don't know it, animals and insects know it. A dog or any animal will obey you as long as you show your authority. But when you become frightened, the dog knows it. Even insects know you are god. This premise was thrust upon my husband as he went to the bathroom.

There was a bug on the ceiling. It probably came in earlier in a bag of groceries and wandered into the bathroom. Lou didn't feel like killing a bug at that time of night. So he said to the bug, "Stay right there and I will see you in the morning."

The following morning, there was the bug, running around in circles on the ceiling waiting to be moved.

Can we influence other's lives with our thought? Absolutely. Scripture says we can bind things on earth and we can loose things on earth. How? With our thought. Often a person will innocently bind a loved one with an unwanted danger by their thinking.

They will say something like, "I love my child so much, I worry all the time. I'm so afraid something awful will happen to him or her."

I tell them, "It certainly could, the way you are thinking."

I explain how powerful our thought is and that there is a cosmic link between us and our loved ones. I show them that we bind them with whatever thought we have concerning them. I teach them to cancel out their old way of thinking—change the picture. To visualize is to actualize. If you are going to bind your loved one with something, make it love, safety, joy and happiness.

I say to them, "Look at the kind of picture you have had about your loved one. That picture spells disaster."

I wrote an article recently about how we pollute our universe with adverse thoughts. Dark energy is heavy. It is our obligation to guard our thoughts and change that darkness into light.

We must send out happy, beautiful vibrations into our universe to cancel out the black ones which have been placed there. These black thoughts, words and actions are too burden-some for Mother Earth. How is she to ascend into the fifth dimension with all that heaviness? When we cancel out a dark thought, we have changed darkness into light which affects literally millions of people.

A client recently told me that she had not been able to enjoy Christmas because of dark feelings. She was mystified when I told her she was possibly picking up that dark energy from someone outside herself. It could have been from someone who had lost a loved one at Christmas time. Of course, I told her that if this happened again, she needed to change that black energy into light.

I said, "You have just become a light-worker in God's army. You may save someone from suicide because, when that dark feeling or thought is changed into light, you have lifted the burden not only for yourself but also for the person from which it came."

Many people get depressed at the holiday season because of the loneliness associated with their loss. Our scientists realize we need more light. They have been trying to design an instrument whereby they can probe the universe to extract light from darkness. One would think a scientist could see the obvious; that the way to do this is through the mind of man. Like magic we can turn darkness into light. When you first try it, it will seem like a miracle. I love miracle stories. Here is one I'd like to share.

A lady told me the story of her son who was in the Vietnam War. His job was to remove the commanders from a battle zone. He rescued them and was on his way out when they were ambushed. Everyone in the vehicle was killed (he thought).

He felt the bullets going right through his body. He kept driving and when he came to a safe place to stop, he was astounded for he had no holes in his body and no blood was evident except in and around his passengers. His mother, at that moment, was thinking of him and praying for his safety.

The following is an example of the power of the mind. A mother saved her son from freezing on the battlefield. He wrote her that it was so cold that he felt he was going to freeze to death. She taught him to meditate and to see himself sitting beside a roaring fire, to actually feel the heat. The son did as she instructed. He did it so proficiently that it actually saved his life; a real miracle.

This next true story is a different kind of miracle, but a miracle nonetheless, from my own experience. It was when money multiplied in my hands. It happened on two different occasions. I went to my broker's office to deposit $500 into my brokerage account. As is their policy, I counted the money, another broker was called in and he counted it and my broker did the same. As we finished the counting, the phone rang.

Ben picked up the phone. Rather than just sit there idle, I picked up the money and began counting it.

I counted out the original $500 and laid the surplus aside. This continued for some time as my broker's eyes got bigger and bigger. He hung up the phone and said, "Why, in the name of God, don't you get a job just counting money!"

This happened once again when I went to the bank to make a deposit. A friend was with me. I had him count the money along with me to make sure it was correct. The teller was busy, so I picked up the money and counted it.

Again there was a surplus. I laid it aside and counted the remainder and again laid the surplus to the side. I counted the money several times and each time there was more than the original deposit. Thank God I always have a witness to these miracles.

I said to God some years ago, "I love these miracles but please make sure I always have a witness. I don't want to doubt my own mind." He has complied with my request, ever since.

DEFINITE STEPS TO ATTAINING WEALTH

Since this book is about manifesting money, I'll relate some real-life experiences. A gentleman was telling me how he could never get ahead, that he could barely pay his bills and put bread on the table. I said to him, "Do you have your billfold with you?"

"Yes, why?" he asked as he reached into his pocket.

"Place it between your hands and repeat after me, 'I bless this money. I send it forth with joy and it returns to me magnified.'"

Then I taught him that when he receives a bill for a service, never to say, "Oh, how am I going to be able to pay these bills?"

Instead say, "I bless these bills and the comfort they represent. I send the payment forth with joy to pay these bills. The money returns to me multiplied."

Then I took one of my business cards in my hand and blessed the card saying, "May this point of contact represent wealth to Jim."

I handed it to him saying, "Each day take this card into your hand and think of riches."

Next I startled him by saying, "I bet you don't tithe."

"What is tithe?" he asked, looking rather startled.

"Ten percent of all you receive should be paid back to God. When you do this, it makes God your partner, and He doesn't ask for fifty percent as most partners would—only ten percent."

"Where do I give it? I can't just throw it up in the sky and say, 'Catch it, God.'"

"You can give some to your church, some to charities or to someone you see in need, or to a source that has given service to you, in a spiritual way. This is your serious money," I answered.

Jim called in a few months to reveal that things were improving mightily. He had received a raise. Next call, he related how he was appointed as manager, which resulted in another substantial raise in salary. Then he and his wife were going on their first vacation in their new car. Then they were able to buy a new house.

I was very pleased at his next call, "Would it be all right to give your card to a friend? He is in the same situation financially as I was when I first met you."

It was a treat as Jim would call every so often to tell me of how his friend was doing exactly as I had instructed and how his prosperity was increasing mightily.

The next call Jim asked if he could come by and have me bless another one of my cards for him because he did not want to lose the magic he had experienced. I answered, "Jim, why don't you bless your own business card in the same way I did mine?"

He was astounded at my suggestion. I finally convinced him that the same God that dwells in me dwells in him. He followed my suggestion and all is still well with Jim.

Another young man to whom I taught this magic called and said, "I have never experienced such magic. My money goes so far. Everything I buy is on sale and I keep getting raises.

"And a man to whom I loaned money who had refused to repay me, chased me down to pay me what he owed me, with interest. I even find money in the streets."

CHAPTER FOUR

Responsibility—Is It Yours?

One more true story comes to mind. A friend came to me in tears. She was really distraught. She had been engaged to a man whom her parents loved. The parents planned a huge wedding.

But then she met Allen and fell head over heels in love with him. She broke her engagement and married Allen. Her fiancée killed himself. Both his and her parents blamed her for his death. Her parents cut her out of the will and disowned her. "Joe's death is all my fault!" she cried in despair.

I shocked her as I said, "Well, I didn't know you had power over life and death. I thought only God had such power."

She straightened her shoulders and said, "Say that again."

I repeated it and she shouted, "You are right. I don't have that kind of power. You have just lifted the world off my shoulders. Thank you."

Several days later she was back. "Now, please help me with another big problem. My husband and I barely make ends meet and my parents whom I love dearly have cut me out of the family and their will. Can you help me with this?"

I gave her the same advice as I had given to Jim and the others which she vowed to follow to the letter. She did, with fantastic financial results. I loved it as she told me how the first time they went to church after my counseling, she said to Allen, "Put ten percent into the collection plate."

Allen retorted, "I can't. I won't have enough to pay the bills."

She insisted; finally saying, "If you don't, I will make a scene." So he complied. He received a raise the next day.

Then I taught her about visualization. I said, "How would you feel if the door bell rang; you went to the door and there stood your parents with outstretched arms welcoming you back into the family?"

She fairly shouted, "That would be heaven!"

I instructed her, "Hold that feeling. It is going to bring you your dream. Just before going to sleep and upon awakening I want you to see that picture with that same sensation."

It didn't take long. She called me, "Guess who is here visiting? My parents! We are having the time of our lives, thanks to you." I informed her it was her faith that brought about the miracle.

But since wealth means fulfillment as well as money, I must continue this story. Susie and Allen were doing so well in the financial realm that they decided to go to Jai Alai and try their luck. Of course they won. As she revealed this, I asked, "Did you pay your tithe on the money you won?"

"What? That is gambling money. But if you say so, I'll do it."

They continued to tithe until ten percent became quite large. One day Allen said, "Look at how much money we are giving away!"

As they began to look at how big their tithe had become, they forgot where it had come from. They began to cut back on their tithe. The very next time they went to Jai Alai, they lost. They continued to lose until they got back to tithing.

Here is another example of visualization with resulting wealth.

A dear one who had been through an impossible marriage and worse divorce was a little skittish at even the thought of another man. Yet she wasn't sure she wanted to spend her life alone. She came to me for counseling. She had been left in dire circumstances by her first marriage.

I told her to start by visualizing the type of man she wanted in her life with all the attributes she desired in a man. Then I asked, "What makes you feel luxurious?"

She replied, "Long bubble baths with a luscious scent, having dinner by candlelight, served in my finest china and crystal—things like that," she replied.

I instructed her, "Visualize doing these things in a majestic setting. Begin now to eat in nothing but your best dinnerware and drink from crystal goblets and treat yourself to long luxurious bubble baths, often."

I instructed her to practice this routine regularly, reminding her of the importance of visualization. I explained, "The best time to visualize your good is just before slumber and upon awakening." She followed my suggestions religiously and today she is married to a most delightful millionaire. Perhaps I should tell you, this beautiful young lady is my daughter.

CHAPTER FIVE

The Devil Made Me Do It

To reiterate: our words, thoughts and visualizations are forceful. We must be ever careful to whom or what we give this kind of power. To paraphrase the late Flip Wilson, "The devil made me do it," or to say it another way, "The devil is responsible for my suffering. In stating this very thing, am I not giving power to the evil forces to make me suffer?"

Why would I give the dark forces power over me? I wouldn't give that kind of power to my dearest friend.

When we blame the devil, Satan, or the dark forces for every adverse thing that happens to us, are we not releasing our power to that dark force?

The scripture says, "In the beginning was the word. The word was with God and the word was God."

Whose word? God's word of course, but also my word, your word; the word creates. Words and thoughts are things; they materialize.

Remember, your thought and certainly your word is a command. Take an example from the dispute you had with your mate. You are so distraught; you think, "I'll go to sleep to forget this terrible fight."

Realizing you cannot think without seeing a picture, what kind of picture is in your mind as you go to sleep? That awful fight, right? Since your subconscious mind's job is to materialize the pictures you put there, you can bet, you and your mate are going to have many more fights. Because that is the picture you are giving your mind to bring to life. It will happen. You say, "How can I keep from materializing this terrible thing?"

Change the film; put in the picture of what you would really like to happen. There is an exact opposite to everything. The opposite of the fight would be you and your mate very much in love, really enjoying your life together.

Think of the happy times you have experienced. Never think of anything you do not want to materialize in your world. Make it a habit to think only of whatever you would love to manifest in your life. It is much more fun to think of a pleasant thing.

When Adam and Eve ate from the tree of knowledge of good and evil, God said, "Now they have become like one of us." What did He mean, like one of us? Now, man can create his own worlds. What are man's building blocks? His words and thoughts.

I have spoken this truth many times, "If you think your world is lined with rainbows, it is. If you think your world stinks, it does." You have created it by your thoughts and words. No one has power over your words and thoughts but you. This is how you express your free will and even the angels in heaven cannot usurp man's free will.

To think of a thing is to give it your very life force. This is what makes it live. To reiterate, "It is your offspring and you are responsible for it." This is where you go back to the chapter in this book that tells you how to change your words and thoughts. Use the club——remember the Masters of the Far East's formula?

God told Abraham, who represents all mankind, "Whatever you see, I promise it to you."

Remember, He did not say it had to be good things you see; the promise was, "Whatever you see, I promise it to you"— good or bad, meaning the picture in your mind.

To manifest wealth you must cleanse your world of all debris, such as allowing yourself to dwell on negative occurrences. If someone has been unfair to you or a loved one has betrayed you, don't give that thing more power to hurt you by thinking of it. It is better that you pray for that person and realize that he or she is living in a human body just the same as you and there may be a reason why this person has betrayed you.

Perhaps the dark forces are trying to bring you down. And just think—if that person did not know you are above them, there would be no reason for trying to bring you down to their level.

Perhaps they have not thought of this truth, "If you must put your foot on someone else to stand tall, you have to be a very small person."

The dark forces know their time is limited and they can only act through the mind of man, so they may try to use any means, even your loved ones, to get at you. Jesus said, "Pray for those who despitefully use you."

When He said,... "Turn the other cheek, and if an enemy asks for your coat, give him your cloak also," He said this for you, not for the one who is doing the dirty deed. Don't waste this precious mind power. We must remove all things that are robbing us of our ability to create wealth.

Negative words, thoughts and feelings cause us to use up this valuable resource. Why waste such a wonderful source of creativity? Put it to use in making your dreams come true.

In my book, *Metaphysical Techniques That Really Work,* I give a technique of how to create and use a power-pak. To double your power to create wealth, use this technique:

When a negative thought, word or deed is manifested, you can pull the power from that negative thing and use it to double your positive power. This is the technique: See the exact opposite of that negative picture.

The faster you turn that negative force around and see the exact opposite of what it is manifesting, the more power you can draw from it. This is why I call it a power-pak.

As an example: You are very angry with your mate. You are thinking of all the ugly things about him or her. And since "like attracts like," you pile up more and more undesirable traits you thought you had forgotten.

You would like to really let him or her have it! To use this power-pak, you do just the opposite of what you would like to do. Say forcefully, "I refuse to let the dark forces get their foot in my door this way."

Then instead of shouting insults, you go over to your mate and tenderly take her in you arms and tell her how much you love and appreciate her. This action knocks the dark forces flat! Now you use the resulting power. You will actually feel twice as powerful as before. Use it to manifest your wealth.

To increase your means of manifesting wealth, it is important to never think of a person or thing that is of lower vibration than yourself. Place your attention on the higher realms, like God, angels, the sun, and emotions like love, beauty, joy, happiness, a beautiful scene or a lovely experience. Choose wisely who you spend your time with, whether in thought or actuality. They can either boost your vibration or tear it down.

Think of great teachers, writers, musicians and great masters. They will strengthen, heal and stimulate you. Chants and mantras have been used successfully for centuries for the purpose of strengthening the psychic or soul energy. They should be sounded in G above middle C. You might add one of these to your daily meditation. Ask your spirit guides and angels to help you.

CHAPTER SIX

Get to Know Your Angels

Scripture says, "You receive not, because you ask not. Ask that your joy may be full." Your angels like to be asked.

You should become familiar with your guides and angels. People often ask me how they can do this. I remember once when I was teaching a class on how to contact your guides. We went into our altered state of consciousness. Since all went well, I had no doubt that everyone had made contact. But to my surprise, no one had or so they said. "Really. None of you met your angel?"

Ignoring this assumption, I said to Terri, "Was your spirit guide male or female?"

"Oh, he was definitely male," she answered without delay.

I asked questions like, "What color was his hair? What style was he wearing? Was his hair long or short?"

"His hair was blonde, about shoulder length and it was straight, combed to one side. His name is Phillip."

I continued around the room asking each student the same type of questions with very positive results. Everyone had made contact with their angel. Why did they not remember at first?

They had returned to their beta consciousness, that work-a-day brain wave frequency that cannot see anything that is not logical. If you cannot touch it, taste it, see it, hear it or sense it, the conscious mind will have nothing to do with it.

Ask yourself, "Is it logical to see angels or spirit guides?" But remember, this beta brain wave constitutes only 5% of your mind. Einstein said that if you can see it, touch it, taste it or sense it, it is most likely an illusion; that the invisible is the real world.

Your subconscious or super-conscious mind, your alpha and theta brain wave frequency comprises the remainder. I call this your "God mind." So what caused the class to finally remember?

I maneuvered the class back to the subconscious by reminding them of their very recent experience. This is why they could then remember. It is important to know that you each have angels. Your angels were assigned to you when you were born. They are always near, but there are ways you can cause them to seem distant. They cannot tolerate disharmony.

My husband and I have noticed that the more we dwell on the presence of angels, like discussing the time and events when we felt their presence, the more we notice their presence. One of my spirit guides gave me a method for helping me with my writing, which has proven to be very helpful. I use it all the time. I was instructed to sit down at my computer and visualize colors swirling around my body. Angels are summoned by colors and by certain sounds. It works.

CHAPTER SEVEN

Every Thought Is a Prayer

Now, back to thoughts. To show you how powerful our thoughts are, try this formula. If I need to get somewhere in a hurry, I project my thoughts to the destination rather than the trip, so no negative programming can set up an obstacle about traffic lights or anything between here and there. I always make it on time.

Someone said, "Every thought is a prayer." Prayer is very important when you are trying to manifest prosperity or anything else in your life. My husband and I recently watched a TV program where a young man who was working for the Peace Corps was instructed to smuggle a large bag of money through a dangerous area. He had notified his father of the perilous journey he would be making.

His father contacted sixteen members of his church and asked them to pray with him for the safety of his son. The young man safely completed his mission. When someone asked the thugs who regularly attack everyone in sight, why they let him go through their area, they replied, "If you had seen those sixteen horrendous warriors with him, you'd know why we left him alone." In actuality, he was alone.

This story exemplifies the Biblical event when Isaiah was about to be attacked by an army. Isaiah had, through clair-audience, been hearing all the plans the king made for attacking the Israelites.

The enemy found this out and decided to kill him. When Isaiah saw the forces coming at him, he prayed that God would reveal His heavenly warriors to the Captain of that army.

God showed them that the mountain was full of horses and chariots of fire. They fled in terror. There is no limit to what God can do when one of His children calls on Him. I heard a minister recently say that each human on earth has, at his or her command, a legion of angels. That amounts to 6000 angels.

Keeping a journal can be a great adventure but it can be a liability if you keep track of negative situations as is shown in the following example. Rose decided to make a journal. She began to keep track of everything, and it took some time before she realized that almost everything she recorded consisted of negative occurrences.

Of course things got much worse because she was focusing on them and most all were negative. She had forgotten that "where attention goes, energy flows." Taking a more constructive approach, she began to record her victories. It was amazing how she began to enjoy her journal as she recorded the positive turn her life had taken. In his book *Wells of Abundance*, E.V. Ingraham states, "My supply is at hand. It fills me, surrounds me and is poured out upon me from everywhere.

"Supply flows to me wherever I am and in whatever I do. My supply is exhaustless and I am richly endowed with all things in Heaven and earth." What a great affirmation to add to your meditation.

God loves for us to appreciate the good He brings into our life. Appreciation is really "praise in action." The more we praise, the more there is to praise. In the metaphysical words of Jesus, "For those who have, more shall be given, and they will have abundance, but to those who have nothing, even what they have shall be taken away."

You say, "That is not fair." But it is a true statement about Universal Law. It shows that those who magnify the loss and hurts in their life shall attract loss and hurt. But those who magnify the good in their lives and give praise for bounty, shall prosper.

It has always been so. We attract what we dwell upon. To condemn is to attract that which you condemn. The Bible says, "With what judgment you judge, you shall be judged." Another way to say it is, "What you resist, persists."

When we focus our attention on the adverse things, we attract them to ourselves. Even the needy help the rich man to prosper.

The poor man looks at his own poverty and dwells on the lack, which attracts more poverty to him. He looks at the wealth of the rich man and thinks how unfair it is for that man to have so much.

His very thought is faith which adds to the rich man's prosperity. The rich man is too busy thinking how he will make the next million to even think of lack, so his wealth multiplies. Sometimes it is good to be redundant to make a point, so excuse me but, the law says, "Whatsoever you sow, that shall you also reap." If you sow thoughts of poverty, you have to reap poverty, but if you sow seed (thoughts) of plenty, you shall reap prosperity.

Emmett Fox tells us that, When we say or imply the word "I" or "I am," we are sowing seeds to the universe and will reap the rewards. If we say, "I am poor, I am ill or I am unhappy," we will reap the dividends of illness, poverty and unhappiness.

But if we say or imply, "I am rich, I am healthy, I am happy," we will reap the rewards of wealth, health and happiness." In Job 22:28 it states, "Thou shall decree a thing and it shall be established unto thee." To decree is to declare or state something. Our very thought is a decree. Think about it!

The old adage of "What the mind of man can conceive and believe, it can achieve," is so true. There are literally millions of things man has not thought of yet, but if he can think of it, he can make it happen. Many situations are set into motion by our thoughts and words.

CHAPTER EIGHT

What You See
Is What You Get

As an example, I pick up a favorite dish. It was given to me by my favorite aunt. I think, "I must not drop this bowl."

So, what happens? I drop that bowl just as if I had planned it. Why? Because of the (thought) picture in my mind of "dropping the bowl." That is the way the mind thinks (in pictures).

You see, what makes the difference is the picture in your mind. You can affirm over and over, "I will never have an accident," but to say even that, you have to see a picture of an accident, right? The picture in your mind is what makes the difference. You might ask, "Then how can I do it otherwise?"

Never use a negative even to denounce a negative. You could say, "I affirm that I will always be a safe and secure driver." Or you could say, "I am safe and secure in all situations." Notice the difference in the picture in your mind?

I place a ring of white light protection around our vehicle every time we use it. I like this method because we reinforce the protection every time we state it. The difference is, you stayed with the positive picture of seeing yourself as a confident driver and you see the picture of protection.

Notice the ways we set up circumstances by the way we think.

When you set a goal, your negative programming immediately sets up barriers like, "What defenses can I institute to make sure nothing keeps me from reaching my goal?"

You begin to think of all the things that can go wrong and you actually set up resistance against achieving your objective. In order to think of all the ifs, ands and buts, you have to see them, and the picture in your mind materializes.

We, not God or circumstances, block our path to prosperity. In the scripture, in 3rd John we read, "Beloved, I wish above all things that you may prosper and be in health, even as your soul prospers." God wants every area of our life to prosper.

CHAPTER NINE

Why Negative Faith Works

Did you know that negative faith works better than positive faith? What happens when you think a negative thought?

A large percentage of the population is backing you up. So when you declare, like my friend Gloria, "I just know this is going to be a terrible day," it will be; for these negative people will believe it right along with her, re-enforcing her negative faith.

I had such a girl in my employ. Ruth loved the salon atmosphere for I did not allow negative conversations in the salon. I insisted on a pleasant, positive salon atmosphere.

But she declared that when she left the salon, nothing went right. I began a positive strategy for Ruth. Each day I would ask her what went wrong after she left the shop, and each day I wrote down the long lists as she enumerated them.

I remember one day I had a list of seventeen things that went wrong. Each day she would end with, ""But, nothing ever goes wrong here, Boss Lady."

One morning as she came bounding into the shop, I turned the tables on her as I asked, "What wonderful things happened after you left the salon last night?"

38

She stopped dead in her tracks. "What? You know nothing ever goes right after I leave here. But I can give you a list of what went wrong."

"No." I answered, "I only want to hear of the good things."

Racking her brain, she replied, "Nothing went right?"

"Oh, I see, your mother-in-law didn't have dinner ready as she usually does?" I inquired.

"Certainly, she did. She always has the meal ready."

"The house was a mess, beds not made, dishes in the sink?"

Looking bewildered Ruth answered, "She is an excellent housekeeper."

"Your husband lost his job?" I continued.

"Of course not. My husband has a very stable position."

"I see; your little boy, Billy, was sick?"

"No, no, he is healthy as a horse."

Much to her surprise, I announced, "Beginning today, we are starting a new program. Each day, I will ask you to tell me everything that went right at home. You may not tell me anything that did not."

At first I had to keep asking questions which required a positive answer as I had done previously. But soon she caught on and she could hardly wait to enumerate the beautiful happenings in her life. This continued for about three months.

One morning she sailed into the salon, ready to relate her many blessings when I stopped her.

"Ruth," I said, "I don't want to hear that today. I want you to tell me of all the things that went wrong."

She thought hard but could not come up with even one negative thing. Finally, she said, "It's strange, but nothing ever goes wrong any more. My life is just wonderful."

I reached in the drawer and pulled out the paper on which I had written the seventeen negative things she had enumerated in one day, several months prior. "This is what you thought was wrong three months ago."

She stood transfixed for a moment. Finally she said, "I can't believe I ever thought like that!"

Then, throwing her arms around me, she exclaimed, "Boss Lady, You tricked me, and I will love you until the day I die for it!"

Here again we learn that "Where your thought goes, energy flows." What is the actual process of how the mind works these things? It is through the pineal gland that we materialize things as if by magic. This pineal gland is the "I am" of the body and is synonymous with the subconscious mind, the right brain and the alpha and theta brain wave frequency.

Human beings originally used this organ to register the finer vibrations, the realm of the ethers.

CHAPTER TEN

The Magic of
the Pineal Gland

As children, we lived much of our lives in a state of magic associated with the pineal gland which was too precious to even share with our parents.

This gland is quite large at birth but it continually diminishes as we become accustomed to the negativity of the world. As we were constantly admonished for our over-exaggerated imagination or just plain tall tales, we learned to disavow our magic ... such as invisible playmates, pets, leprechauns and floating on clouds. How sad to lose the magic of when a toy truck became a monstrous earth-moving machine, when a doll was a real live baby, and our comfort blanket was a magic carpet that could whisk us to faraway mysterious places.

My sister would ram her hands into the pockets of her jeans and spin tales of her exploits when she was big. When Joseph of the Bible tried to share his visions with his brothers, they chided, "Behold here cometh the dreamer." Joseph replied, "Without dreams and visions the people perish."

Growing to adulthood—when the pineal gland had diminished to the size of a pea—we gave up the magic and joined the negative world. By the time we were six years old, we had heard the word, "no" 60,000 times.

Realizing what we have lost, and as we become wiser, we spend a great deal of our time trying to get back the magic, through transcendental meditation, awareness programs, working with the right brain and altered states of consciousness.

We spend time learning about brain wave frequencies and the subconscious mind. We now understand why Jesus of the Bible said, "Except ye become as little children, ye shall not see the kingdom of God." He was referring to the pineal gland and the theta brain wave frequency which opens our minds to the kind of magic we once knew as children.

It is as if, having recently descended from that celestial realm when we were born, we retain some of the wonderment of the Godhead.

Like Plato, who talked of the soul coming from a higher, divine realm of being, he believed that birth begins the sleeping and forgetting. The soul goes from a state of acute awareness to a much less conscious state and therefore forgets the truths we knew before birth. He implied that death is an awakening, a remembering.

I am reminded of a cartoon where a small boy is shaking his newborn baby sister and saying, "Please, tell me about God and Heaven. It has been so long, I am about to forget."

CHAPTER ELEVEN

The Magnificent Power That You Are

Yet, we as adults have taken control of the electrical energy, "which is what we are composed of" and have materialized a home and furnishings, cars, vacations and also our misfortunes.

We should know by now that universal substance is everywhere present, just waiting for us to take it and, with our thoughts, mold it into whatever we desire.

Just think of how you do this every day! You begin with an idea, a picture in your mind. It might be a new car. You begin to notice other cars just like the one in your mind. You meander down to the dealer and take that car for a spin. By now you know the color, the model and how it feels to drive it. You begin to visualize owning that car.

You are in the process of molding universal substance. The electrical energy "which is you" begins a process of materialization. And one day, almost like magic, you are driving that very car. The magic of it all is that everything is formulated from the same substance as your new car. Nothing can happen until someone thinks about it. Your body, your children, your home, plants and animals are all the same ... energy operating at different frequencies.

It is all molecules of energy. Energy cannot die and so nothing is dead—not even the chair you are sitting on. Everything is alive. Everything is energy. I repeat, "Energy cannot die"—it can only transform into another type of energy. Everything on this earth, if subjected to enough heat, will be reduced to energy.

Put these fragments under the microscope, and you will find one thing only: light. Light is energy and the Bible says that God is light or, in other words, God is everything that exists.

In your materialization you took from the ethers, molecules of energy and transformed them into a new car. It all began as an idea in you mind. The only difference between that new car and your body or a plant is the rate of vibration of these molecules.

You do this every day when you awaken and plan your day. You get out of bed and shave or apply your make-up, have breakfast and go to the office. Do you realize that none of this could have happened if you had not thought about it?

You just manifested the way you materialize everything in your life. The moment you begin to think, you are molding universal substance, molecules of energy. Einstein called it $E=mc^2$—something from nothing and nothing from something.

The raw materials are molecules of energy and your thought which transformed them into that new car and a brand new day.

Without these two magical components, nothing could have happened. Are you beginning to understand why Jesus said, "Know ye not that ye are gods?" We are indeed co-creators with God and we are creating all the time, either consciously or subconsciously.

Even as we sleep, we are creating—which is why at four AM, my subconscious mind created this article. We haven't advanced in spirit like Jesus, who instantaneously materialized bread and fish to feed 5000 people on several occasions and had a gold coin to appear in the mouth of a fish to pay the taxes.

Or like Sai Baba of India, who materialized gold and other objects in mid-air and had them fall into the hands of his audience—but we are doing it in a minuscule way; it just takes longer.

God is pleased when we use our minds and talents to manifest whatever we need to make us happy. Notice how the scripture praises riches and declares they are all of God. In Psalms 104:24 it says, "Oh, Lord, how manifold are thy works! In wisdom has thou made them all; the earth is full of thy riches."

But have you ever had the feeling that you are not worthy of having riches? In Ecclesiastes 5:18 we read, "Behold that which I have seen; that it is good and comely for one to eat and to drink and to enjoy the good of his labour that he taketh under the sun all the days of his life, which God giveth him, for it is his portion."

And 5:19 states, "Every man also whom God hath given riches and wealth and hath given him power to eat thereof, and to take his portion and to rejoice in his labour; this is the gift of God."

And in Proverbs 14:24 it says, "The crown of the wise is their riches; but the foolishness of fools is folly."

Psalms 45:4 gives this counsel, "In majesty ride prosperously because of truth, meekness and righteousness."

We must learn how to become an evolved human being. An evolved person is free from traits like craving attention, awards and recognition. An evolved person doesn't have to prove anything to anyone and never thinks the world owes him something. He never feels jealous, guilty, or possessive.

And he doesn't need to react to things. If someone insults an evolved person, he sees it as the other person's problem.

Wouldn't it be great to work as if you don't need money, love as if you've never been hurt, and dance as if no one is looking?

A great thought: If we continue to think the way we've always thought, we'll continue to get what we've always gotten. We have made our worlds what they are today.

Fear is probably the greatest one thing that holds us back, that prevents us from becoming the great beings we were meant to be.

Fear hinders us from attaining wealth as we should. Luke 12:32 says, "Fear not, little flock, for it is your Father's good pleasure to give you the kingdom."

We find the answers to many of our challenges in the scriptures. Even the scientists have learned to search the Bible for answers as in the following example.

SCIENCE FINDS LOST DAY

Harold Hill of Baltimore, Maryland, a consultant with the space program, checked space to determine where the sun, moon and planets would be 100 and 1000 years from now. This information is imperative because, when sending up future satellites, we must make sure that they do not bump into anything while in orbit, many years from now.

He ran the computer measurement back and forth over the centuries and found that something was drastically wrong. There was a day missing in space! One member of the team remembered that the Bible spoke of the sun standing still. In the book of Joshua, it told that when Joshua's army was surrounded by the enemy, if darkness fell, his army would be overpowered.

Joshua asked God to cause the sun to stand still. "And the sun stood still and the moon stayed and hasted not to go down about a whole day," Joshua 10:8,12–13.

The computers were checked, going back in time. The lapsed time amounted to 23 hours and 20 minutes, not quite a whole day. With 40 minutes unaccounted for, there could still be trouble 1000 years from now.

A closer examination of the Bible revealed that the answer was to be found in 2nd Kings. Hezekiah, while on his death bed, was visited by Isaiah, the prophet. Isaiah informed Hezekiah that he was not going to die. God honored Hezekiah's request for a sign by having the sun's shadow turn backward ten degrees. It was learned that 10 degrees backward amounted to exactly 40 minutes, making a total of 24 hours. Science had found the lost day.

"Psychotronics" was a new word which I added to my vocabulary recently. The word came about when a group of scientists were studying matter at the microscopic level to prove the equation: Science + Spirit = Evolution or in other words, "Interaction of matter, energy and consciousness equals manifestation."

As an example, one of the scientists believes that love coupled with consciousness affects our DNA.

Dr. Lou Childre was able to prove his theory three consecutive times from a distance of a mile.

We have a tendency to think of matter as being solid, but in reality, there is no such theory. We tend to view the invisible as if it did not exist. As stated earlier in this book, Einstein believes the invisible is the real world.

Ancient man was more attuned to the spirit of things than we are today, as delineated by Native American drawings on the walls of their caves, images of animals with human heads or human bodies with animals' heads. Because when they ate the meat of an animal, it gave them life, the animal was thought of as a god. We think of our food as solid, yet when we eat it and it is digested (giving us life), any portion that is not changed into invisible energy or life force is evacuated by the body.

Everything has a spiritual counterpart. The space around us seems to be empty, but it is abundant with invisible things. Think of it: when a scientist takes from the invisible elements one part oxygen and adds two parts hydrogen, he comes up with water. Another example is when water is frozen, it becomes ice.

I'm attempting to show you that if we can think deeply enough, we will realize that nothing is impossible, that God made it possible to demonstrate wealth or whatever we wish.

These same scientists found that when DNA samples were placed in front of healers, with unconditional love, the helix unwound faster. The electromagnetic force field, which we call the aura, is affected by visualization, which is used in healing; again it is psychotronics at work, the interaction of consciousness, matter and energy.

Remember the healing that took place when cancer patients were taught to visualize the fighter cells as pac-man eating up the cancer cells? It worked. One of the scientists went so far as to suggest that molecular electronics has the capability to cure physical ills by using a holographic image of a drug rather than the drug itself.

As we have known for some time, we are all primarily tiny electrically charged particles called protons and electrons, held together by electrical attraction. Remember how absurd it seemed when we first heard of painting electrical circuits instead of using wires? It probably seemed as flagrant as proving that a holographic image could be as effective as the drug itself or that an invisible element, like love could affect our DNA. Miracles happen every day. Why not your miracle?

The people we associate with will definitely have a profound effect on whatever we are trying to manifest in our lives.

We must be very careful who we share our miracle with. Do not tell anyone about it who might doubt it. They can have a negative effect on the outcome. I believe this is why, when Jesus did His miracles, he said, "Go and tell no man." He did not want their negative faith to interfere.

Do you know that negative faith works better than positive faith? Why? Because 80% of the population is backing up the negative faith. When someone says, "This is going to be a horrible day," 80% of the people are believing it, with him.

I told a friend of what a sneaky God we serve. He looked shocked for a minute. I continued, "He sneaks His miracles and blessings in on us without warning. If He can do this, then I can do sneaky prayers. I do this a lot. This way I can keep negative faith from interfering with my healing programs."

CHAPTER TWELVE

Psychic Vampires

Have you ever heard of psychic vampires? Who are they? Psychic vampires are very negative people who have so little psychic energy that they are in constant search of people of high psychic energy so they can drain it for their own benefit, although some are unaware of doing this. But they can do just as much harm. How will you know if you are in the presence of a psychic vampire?

You will feel completely drained. I will give a true example. I'll change the name for the sake of privacy. Shirley was a minister with a large following. I worked with her organization for a time.

I noticed that both Shirley and her Executive Director, Rob, at times seemed completely drained of all energy. I decided I must find the cause of this problem. It came to my attention that every time Shirley would dictate a letter to her secretary, Gloria, she had to go lie down. I also noticed the same type of effect when the secretary was in the presence of her Executive Director.

Rob had just returned from having lunch with Gloria. He looked as if he could drop in his tracks. This was enough for me to begin my search. In about a week I went into Shirley's office and made this announcement. "Shirley, you have a psychic vampire in your midst."

"What in the world is a psychic vampire?" she inquired.

"It is someone who drains your psychic energy. Have you noticed that every time you are around your secretary, you have to lie down?"

"I do have to lie down a lot, but I hadn't considered the cause. I just thought I was depleted for some reason."

"It is imperative that you release that secretary. Your health and that of your Executive Director is at stake." She took my advice and in no time she and Rob were feeling great.

If you must be in the presence of a psychic vampire or anyone who might have an adverse affect on you, place a cylinder of light as protection around you.

To some of you this is elementary, but I have found students who had not the slightest idea of how to do this, especially if they were not adept at visualization. Let me explain.

To visualize, one must compare it to the way you think. As stated earlier in this book, you cannot think of anything without seeing a picture. Try it! It is impossible. And remember, we do not see in flat pictures as if looking at a photograph. When we think, we see in three-dimensional pictures. Think of a loved one and notice how you see every feature—you can even hear how they speak or laugh. This is visualization.

This is how you see things in your mind to manifest wealth or whatever you are trying to materialize. We might call it imagination. People often ask, after experiencing a miracle such as seeing an angel, "How can I be sure it is not just my imagination?"

I tell them, "It is your imagination. Without the image, you have nothing. Imagination is our greatest gift from God."

CHAPTER THIRTEEN

Our Most Powerful Tool

Without imagination we could never manifest wealth or anything else we are wanting to materialize in our lives.

The most powerful things cannot be seen, but we know they exist. You can't see the wind, but you can feel it. We don't understand electricity, but we use it every day. We have not seen God nor Jesus, but we know they exist. How? Our imagination, which is how we visualize or see with our third eye. If you want to experience angels, get your imagination working. In no time you will see and experience angels.

I met an extraordinary man from India recently. His name is Sri Anand, man of miracles. I was healed by him. He studied and worked with the great Master, Sai Baba. I asked him if I could have the privilege of relating some of his miracles to my readers.

He and I know that the fact that you can desire a thing is evidence that it should be yours. One day he was at a certain business admiring some expensive statues of the Madonna, some great Masters, etc. The artist came over and asked if he would like to purchase one of them. He very emphatically said, "No, I would like for you to donate one to my Ashram."

She was taken aback for an instance and then replied, "Select one you like and it is yours."

Looking over the huge selection, he replied, "I'd really like that large one over there, but I will take this one which is about all I can carry. Thank you."

The scripture, "Ask and it shall be given you, seek and you shall find, knock and it shall be opened unto you," is phenomenal in its clarity if one believes the scripture.

I do not know where I learned the following technique for manifesting whatever you desire. But for so many years I have used it to manifest many miracles in my life and have since introduced it to others. I began teaching it in my Treasure-mapping classes.

I use a 3 by 5 card, which is numbered down one side. At the bottom I write, "It is done," and leave one line for a signature.

On the other side I write, "Ask and it shall be given you, seek and you shall find, knock and it shall be opened to you." At the bottom I left room for a signature and add "So be it!"

On the numbered slots you write an item you would like to manifest. You must always sign your name on each side. This has served me well for many years. When I decided to share this with others, to prove it really works, I chose to make it so difficult that it was near to impossible.

I wrote 17 things that I wanted—things I had never been able to manifest before, such as how much money I could have in my savings and checking accounts in a given period of time, a new car, a full carat diamond, an outrageous vacation and on and on.

I drew a line through each item as it materialized. Within six months I had marked off everything on my list. I have used it in conjunction with my treasure-mapping classes ever since. It is a good practice for materializing whatever you want from life.

Sometimes we need to look beneath the surface to find the real gold. A good example is artist Richard Wawro (pronounced Vavro) of Edinburgh, Scotland, a genius yet he is legally blind, autistic, diabetic and severely retarded. He had sold more than 1000 of his pictures by age 31.

He is slight build, has blue eyes and unruly brown hair. By age two he had had four operations on his eyes. He barely slept three hours a night. His yelling, screaming and jerking nearly drove his mother insane. Her husband insisted that she go back to teaching and have someone else take care of Richard.

They found a gentle, patient woman who would take the job. Richard's doctors felt they should institutionalize him.

When he was six, he was fitted with thick lens glasses. Even then he could barely see if he was very close to the object.

The parents took him for an interview with Molly Leisman, an artist/teacher. The suffering in his face caused her to accept him into the Occupation Center.

His piercing screams disturbed the other children and many times she was tempted to give up on Richard. But one day she put a crayon in his hand and watched as he made strong lines on the page. She gave him many colors and he became absorbed in the seeming magic. When she returned to see what he would do with the crayons, she was amazed! She took some samples of Richard's drawings to her artist husband without telling him who had done them. He told her that the child had talent beyond his years.

A new world of peace and fulfillment slowly opened to Richard. When he was twelve, Marian Bohusz Szyszko, founder of the Polish School of Art in London, examined Richard's drawings. He was thunder-struck! The drawings were "an incredible phenomenon" rendered with the precision of a mechanic and the vision of a poet.

When he was seventeen, an entire room was used to display twenty of his pictures. He sold eight of them. He usually works over a counter with his head six to eight inches from the paper. Like most autistics, he has difficulty articulating ideas and feelings. Sometimes he overcomes this by saying, "I can see feeling good."

It took a tremendous person like Molly Leisman to search and find the gold which might never have been discovered except for her dedication which was invested in Richard Wawro.

I'll relate to you the story of one of my former students who knew to look for the gold but only after a little reminder. Lorene was one of my students. But if she stayed away from class for too long, she seemed to forget the things she learned. As long as I was constantly instructing her, she could demonstrate miracles, but if she didn't see me for a while, she ceased her metaphysical work.

On this particular day, she came to my door and said, "I desperately need a miracle and I must have your help."

"Lorene, after all the miracles in your life, how could you need me or anyone to bring them about?" I asked.

"I really need a washer and dryer and I have no money and no credit," she informed me.

Handing her a pencil and pad, I instructed her, "Okay, Lorene, let's get back to basics. Let's treasure-map for your miracle. Draw a picture of a washer and dryer or a reasonable facsimile of one," I instructed.

"I'm not an artist. I can't draw a washer or dryer."

"Then draw two blocks and write on one 'washer' and on the other 'dryer.' You should remember the other steps," I said.

"I'm ashamed to admit it, but I don't remember."

"Do you only do your metaphysical work when you need something? Lorene, you must remember that it is just as impor-

tant to 'prove Him' when you do not need anything. Now let's
get on with your miracle. On the bottom of the picture, write,
'This or something better, Father' and sign your name. And you
must remember that when you sign your name, it becomes a
contract," I instructed.

Fumbling with the pencil, she said, "Oh, I remember that,
but for the life of me I can't remember why it is a contract."

"Lorene, in treasure-mapping (scientific prayer), you are so
sure that God will fulfill your desire that you sign a contract with
Him. This is why it takes more faith than the usual way of
praying and asking for something. Do you believe that much,
right now, enough to sign a contract?" I asked.

"How could I not believe, after the many times it has
worked for me in the past? Of course, I believe! That's why I'm
here."

As she left, I reminded her to look at the picture often with
the exuberance and pride of ownership, and not to think about
where it would come from.

The very next day, I had a call from a friend. She did not
know Lorene nor of her need for a washer and dryer.

Sue asked, "Do you know of anyone who could use a washer
and dryer? We are replacing all the appliances at our laundry
business and I want to give them as tithe to someone as a token
of our thanks to God for the success of our business."

I immediately called Lorene. She was not surprised as she
had seen miracles as a result of treasure-mapping before, but she
was flabbergasted at how fast it happened. Lorene was lax when
it came to doing what she knew, but her faith was up to par.

The promise is, "Whatever you believe if you do not doubt,
it shall be yours," or words to that effect.

Shouldn't Lorene feel wealthy, knowing she can achieve
miracles? What constitutes "being rich?" I have been asked
many times, "Are you wealthy?"

Usually I have to answer with a question, "Compared to who or what?" If you compare me to Bill Gates or some other billionaire, I'd have to answer, "No." But compared to a third world citizen, I would definitely say, "Yes."

CHAPTER FOURTEEN

A Definition of Wealth

I ran across this internet article that probably answers that question better than I. It was titled, "No Subject," but it seems to me a good definition of wealth. It went like this:

If you woke up this morning with more health than illness ... you are more blessed than the million who will not survive the week.

If you have never faced the danger of battle, loneliness of imprisonment, the agony of torture, or pangs of starvation ... you are ahead of 500 million people in the world.

If you can attend a church meeting without fear or harassment, arrest, torture, or death ... you are more blessed than three billion people in the world.

If you have food in the refrigerator, clothes on your back, a roof overhead and a place to sleep ... you are richer than 75% of this world.

If you have money in the bank, in your wallet, and spare change in a dish somewhere ... you are among the top 8% of the world's wealthy.

If your parents are still alive and still married ... you are very rare, even in the United States.

If you hold your head up with a smile on your face and are truly thankful ... you are blessed because the majority can, but most do not.

If you can hold someone's hand, hug them or even touch them on the shoulder ... you are blessed because you can offer God's healing touch.

If you can read this message, you just received a double blessing in that someone was thinking of you.

And furthermore, you are more blessed than over two billion people in the world that cannot read at all. Have a great day and count your blessings.

Wealth can come through when the barriers are removed, but they must first be brought to the surface. The following is a good example of how to do this.

HIDDEN GUILT MUST BE BROUGHT TO SURFACE

A client brought her friend, a banker (we'll call him Mr. Smith) to me for counseling. He said, "Every day millions of dollars pass through my hands, yet I have not the power to get rid of this excruciating pain that plagues me day and night. I have not slept more than an hour at a time in twenty years because of this horrible pain."

I was very psychic, I believe as a result of having died and was brought back to life. No one's life can remain the same after such a forceful experience. I saw this man's suffering.

I said, "A piece of metal went right through your chest, but that healed seven years ago. That cannot be the reason for your pain."

I began to see into his past and I said, "The guilt is from the two men that you killed."

He said, "Oh, my God that is it. I had buried that horrible thing so far into my subconscious that I did not even remember it. That is the reason for my pain. It is guilt."

I saw still deeper and I said, "Wait just a minute. I see that this killing was in defense of your country. That is not the reason for your guilt."

He said, "I know that is it. It has to be why I am suffering. And no wonder, it is from this awful guilt."

I said, "No, there is a deeper reason. The guilt is because, you not only killed these two men, you enjoyed watching them die!"

He threw his hands over his face, "Oh, My God, you are right. I actually stood over those men and enjoyed watching them die. No wonder I have been suffering all these years. What a monster I am! I must suffer the rest of my life for what I have done."

I said, "There is an answer. You can ask God to forgive you and then forgive yourself, and you can be set free from this guilt and pain."

He said, "Oh, no, I cannot ever forgive myself for such a hideous thing."

I told him, "When God casts your sins from you as far as the east is from the west to be remembered no more, that is the end of it."

He said, "That is not the end of it. I cannot forgive myself."

I answered, "If you hold that guilt against yourself after God has forgiven you, you are trying to make yourself bigger than God and you are not."

By now he was quite angry with me and he practically ran away from me shouting over his shoulder, "I'm sorry I ever met you, doctor. I never want to see you again."

I finished my business in that city and had just gotten home as the phone was ringing. My client was trying to reach me. She said, "I have to tell you about the banker I brought to you. After he left, the words, 'What makes you bigger than God,' rang in his ears until he asked God to forgive him. Then he forgave himself. He hasn't had a pain since and he sleeps like a baby, and he's back once more enjoying his position as banker."

Earl Nightingale, when asked to define what it meant to be wealthy, replied, "The man who does what he wants to do, only when he wants to do it and only because he wants to do it, is wealthy."

I have known thirteen millionaires and each one of them attained their wealth by using metaphysical principles.

Some of them did not know the word, "metaphysics," but somehow they put the universal law into effect without knowing how they did it and, since the law is irrefutable, it worked.

To emulate the wealthy man, one might think of Napoleon Bonaparte, who was once the Emperor of France. When he decided to become Emperor, people laughed at him: "An emperor only five foot tall?" they scorned.

But Napoleon knew of the Universal Law. He knew that if he could convince himself that he could be Emperor, it would indeed be so. He hired an actor to teach him how to look like an Emperor, walk and talk like an Emperor, how to dress like an Emperor; he asked, "What would an Emperor eat?... How would he mount a horse?"

He lived the life of an Emperor every waking moment and dreamed of it by night. By the time he felt like an Emperor, he was indeed the Emperor of France.

We've all heard the cliché, "Fake it till you make it." Strive to become that person who never gripes nor slanders another.

Become a man or woman who never lets himself be controlled by another's comments; who never gives anyone power to make him angry or feel less than he is; one who gives no one a reason to be his enemy, who never talks about himself unless it is necessary ... and never boastfully.

Before he expresses his opinion about anything, he makes sure he knows all the facts and is never afraid to say "I don't know."

He can never be poor or miserable, for come what may, in his heart he remains happy and prosperous. This man is at peace with himself and presumes a quiet sense of purpose. He does not fear anyone nor anything. He maintains a positive mental attitude and is slow to accuse, quick to forgive and makes allowances for others.

This man would never give his power to another, which reminds me of an article I wrote recently. I entitled it: "Give My Power to Who???"

I was watching a TV program where a minister was blaming the devil for all his ills.

I thought, "Why would anyone give the devil power to make him/her suffer? I wouldn't give that kind of power to my best friend!"

You might ask, "How do I give my power to anyone or anything?"

You do it by giving a situation or a person the power to make you angry, or to make you feel inferior.

You give away your power by giving anyone or anything the most precious thing you can call your own—your thought, which is your very life force.

To express it another way, "The devil is responsible for my suffering." What am I doing but giving the devil power over my problem, even my life? Why allow the dark forces into your world in the first place? You invite them in by acknowledging they exist. Nothing can come into your world unless you admit it.

A good analogy: the door bell rings. You go to the door. Whoever is standing there is waiting for you to admit him or turn him away. It is strictly up to you. One good way to know you are giving your power away is when you get that certain queasy feeling in the pit of your stomach. You do this through your thought and your word.

Words and thoughts are things; they materialize.

God gave us free will, and even the angels cannot take that away from us. I have said many times, "If you think your world stinks, it does, but if you think your world is lined with rainbows, it is." You have made it what it is, by your thoughts. No one has control over your words and thoughts but you. To think of a thing is to give it your very life force! You give it life. You make it live. Never, never think of anything unless you want it to materialize in your world. I make this point over and over in my book *Metaphysical Techniques That Really Work*.

Most of us were taught that to cry over or worry about our loved ones is indicative of being a good friend or parent. But I declare unto you that is the worst thing you can do to anyone. You actually bind that person with whatever you are worrying about concerning them. Place them into God's hands and trust Him to take care of them. If you begin to worry about that loved one, you have taken him/her out of God's hands and placed him back into your own. Whose hands would you rather have them in, yours or God's?

I hear so often, "Teach me how to place a protective light around my dear one."

I explain that it is much like a thought. To reiterate, you cannot think without seeing a picture.

See in your mind's eye a cylinder of light surrounding you and your loved ones. Each time you do this you re-enforce the light.

Remember the scripture that says, "Whatever you see, I promise it to you." God did not say it had to be good things you see. The promise is: "Whatever you see, good or bad, I promise it to you."

So be careful what you see, for it shall be yours.

The scripture says it this way, "Be careful what you set your heart upon, for you shall surely have it."

You again ask, "What does this have to do with giving my power away?" When you worry (that is, see a negative picture), that is exactly what you are doing? You have the power to see a good thing or a bad thing, to smile or frown, to trust God or give in to the dark forces. Which will you choose?

It is our responsibility to change darkness into light at every opportunity. If a dark thought or feeling invades your consciousness, you must change it into light.

YE ARE GODS

Everything in your world is whatever you think it is. If you think your world is lined with rainbows it is; if you think it stinks, it does. Your thoughts have made it so. The power of thought is the highest power in the universe. Though it has always been so, science has just recently discovered that the power of thought is as strong as the thing one is thinking about. For instance, they found that if one would think powerfully that he or she has taken a specific medication, though he had not, the body will react as though it had.

I saw the results of such action when my husband forgot to take his heart medication which he had relied on for years. In the past when he forgot to take this pill, he had serious ramifications until he could go back home and take it. This time when he forgot to take his medication, I explained this to him. He put a powerful thought into his mind that he had indeed taken the pill and his symptoms ceased. It may be necessary for you to do this in steps.

First (in your mind) see the pill in your hand. Then visualize putting the pill in your mouth. Next see a glass of water as you raise it to your lips. Finish this by taking a drink of water as the pill is washed down with the water. You might even gulp. See how easy it works!

In my book *Metaphysical Techniques That Really Work* I expound on the fact that the subconscious mind does not know the difference between a real and an imaginary experience. If you can imagine (think of) it, it can happen. I remember reading about a monk high in the mountains alone, who knew this truth. He was lonely. So he used his subconscious mind and each day would visualize a big fat yogi sitting with him keeping him company each day. Sure enough, on a particular day, a big fat yogi appeared and stayed with him for several years.

The power of thought is so powerful that when planted in the subconscious mind, it can produce results in the present or in the future.

When we are trying very hard to do something, we are using our little 5% beta consciousness. A friend called to tell me he could not find his car keys. He had searched every inch of his home but came up empty.

I told him to get his mind off of the car keys and get busy doing something else that required all his attention. Why? As you get involved in something else, which requires that beta consciousness (the 5%) mind, this gets the little guy out of the way. Remember, when you are trying, it is him that you are using.

The subconscious—that other 95% of your mind—will take over and you will know where your keys are without thinking about it. He followed my advice. In about five minutes he had his car keys in his hand.

Your theta brain wave frequency knows no limits. It is your 95% subconscious mind that does not know the difference between a real and an imaginary experience. This part of your mind knows what Jesus taught even if you do not. Jesus said, "Know ye not that ye are Gods?"... speaking of that subconscious mind. God told us that He made us in his own image, His very own likeness.

I will share my poem, "His Image, His Likeness," with you at the end of this message. When we become enlightened to where we can believe this, we can have miracles happening without number.

It is that little %5 beta consciousness that gets us into trouble. This part of our mind is very important in that it controls all our senses. Leave it to that. It is good to get this part of your mind on some task that requires you to really work at it.

This leaves your theta consciousness free to do the work that the beta consciousness knows nothing about. It is very important to realize that when you are trying, you have slipped back into your little beta consciousness (that 5% part of your mind).

The subconscious—that 95% of your brain wave frequency—the theta brain waves need no effort on your part. This is the easy path. All you really need to do is get very relaxed and place a picture in your mind of what it is you wish to accomplish. Einstein used this method all his life for his great accomplishments. He would place all the information he knew about the task at hand and then he would take a five-minute nap.

When he awoke, he had the answer. This is where the advice, "Sleep on it" came from.

To know when you are in your theta brain wave frequency, remember when you were a child and you stared out the window, not seeing anything ... just being ... no strain, no worry, just knowing all is well? That's the feeling.

This is your most powerful self. This is why your dreams come true. As you are dozing off, you are in your theta brain wave frequency; this is the time to think of all the great things you want to accomplish. We must be careful of our thoughts. Remember words and thoughts are things. They materialize.

"Whatsoever a man soweth, that shall he also reap." That scripture did not say it had to be good seeds you sow. The admonition is, "Whatever you sow." But the promise is the same regardless, whatever you sow, you will reap. So be aware of your words and thoughts.

The following incident shows how this works. A friend shared with me this series of actions. As she and her husband sat at breakfast one morning, he looked out the window at his private plane and remarked, "Look at that fence. Wow! If I ever came in just a little too low, I could lose a wing."

So the very next time he flew his plane, guess what? He came in a little too low and ripped off a wing. His wife delighted in telling me how she couldn't wait to say to him, "You really set that one up, didn't you?"

We really are "Little Gods." Everything is what you think it is. If you don't know it, just watch how everything in our world knows it. Your thoughts are so powerful that you can curse a plant or flower and it will wither up and die. But you can also love and bless the same and they will thrive and grow.

In a Mind Science class we were testing such theories and proving them. We tested it on a fly that had gotten into the classroom. To prove a point we each visualized that fly coming and perching on the tip of a finger. We proved it over and over.

A weed knows of our control over it. I watched a weed try hard to look like a nearby plant so I would not cut it down. It worked. I let that weed continue to grow because it even changed its color, and then took on the shape of the leaves of the other plant.

Trees, especially pines with long needles, will share their energy if you ask them. I knew of a gentleman who had tuberculosis and had only a few months to live. He had heard of the healing power of pine trees, so he took a tent and camped out in a pine forest. In six months he went back to his doctor who pronounced him totally healed. How could this happen? It is no mystery. God put all His creation under man's dominion. Everything has to bow to man if man handles it with respect.

Why doesn't it work every time? It all goes back to how much you can believe in man's dominion. Can you believe that you really are that powerful—that you can command God's creation and it will obey you?

I remember reading of a very spiritual man who gave account of how he laughed at a recent hurricane as it tried to attack his home. He stood in his house and made fun of the hurricane, actually laughed as it tried to demolish his domain. He took dominion! The hurricane actually picked his house up off its foundation and, as he laughed all the harder, it set the house right back down on the foundation with no damage.

Have you ever suddenly had a feeling of almost desperation and could not figure where it was coming from? If you will tune into your intuitive mind, you can usually tell from where it is coming. Someone is sending out a strong signal. In such a case, one should get very quiet and listen to that still, small voice. Send a Christ Light in the direction from where you feel the catastrophe. It works.

Never worry about anyone. To worry only binds the person with the condition with which you are concerned. What can a person do that will help and not hurt one you want to help? You visualize that person with the exact opposite condition. If he or she is ill, you visualize the exact opposite. See that one as healthy. If the condition is one of lack, see him or her surrounded with the things needed.

It is better that you not even think of that one than to worry about them. Wayne Dyer often says, "You can never get sick enough to heal one person. You can never hurt enough to cure one person, and you can never be sad enough to cure one person's worry." Dyer says that if you should call his number and get his answering service, this is the message you will hear: "I intend to be happy. If you have any other thing in mind, you have the wrong number."

The poem I promised to share:

HIS IMAGE, HIS LIKENESS

Recently while dwelling on my limitations, this message came to me: GOD was saying, "Don't blaspheme me. And don't call me a liar! You are not limited. I made you in my own Image; My Likeness.

"You are perfect because you are my creation, my child, and I love you as only a Heavenly Father could love you!

"I care not what you did thirty years ago, ten years ago, yesterday, nor the last minute. As of now, this second, you stand before me my perfect child.

"How can it be otherwise? You cannot live in the past nor in the next moment. You can live in the only time you have, which is NOW.

"Yesterday is gone forever and you can do nothing about it. Tomorrow never comes. You are responsible for only this moment: NOW.

"All your sins of the past are cast as far from you as the East is from the West, to be remembered no more. At this moment, the only time you have, you have not sinned, not in the future, for it is not here. Yesterday is gone forever. This, my child is eternity.

"You are unlimited. There are no chains that bind you. At this moment, the only time you have, you are my perfect child: My Image, My Likeness."

Your life's work should be something you love so much, that you would do it for nothing, but you get paid very well for it. I have always believed that one should play as much as one works. If this seems impossible, then make your work seem like play. My mother had a knack for making work seem like a playful adventure.

When the comforters and blankets needed laundering and we had no washing machine, she still made it pay off. She would fill the large tub with warm soapy water and put the bedclothes into it. Then she would call to us children, telling us that we could take turns, two at a time, stomping them with our bare feet. We each looked forward to our turn. We did indeed enjoy it.

When she would wax the linoleum floors, we were privileged to take turns at skating on them with soft cloths under our feet to make them shine. Mother always taught us that "What you do, do with your might, and if you are not going to put your heart and soul into whatever you do, don't do it." She could always smile or laugh at the slightest provocation. She liked to quote the scripture, "Make a joyful noise unto the Lord."

I owned beauty salons for many years. In sharing with each other, my clients often told of how they could hardly wait for Friday to come so they could be off from work.

Seeing how distasteful their present employment was, I often asked why they didn't quit and find another more pleasing situation. The answer was always, "I can't afford to change jobs."

I had to answer that I could not see how they could afford not to.

Manifesting wealth also includes knowing how to handle your finances.

DOWN TO EARTH ADVICE

I have counseled many who have had no formal training in how to handle credit cards and interest. I recall when my son was a teenager; we decided to see if we could trust him with a credit card. We found that at that time, we could not. He was going around treating all his friends to a full tank of gas and putting things on the credit card that should not be. So, of course we withdrew his credit card. I'm thankful that today he thinks like his mother. One should collect interest and never pay it unless absolutely necessary.

I have had credit cards all my adult life, but I have never paid interest. When the bill comes due, I pay it in full: no interest.

My husband had never learned that lesson until I came into his life. He, like most Americans, paid the minimum charge on his credit card and he owned a mortgage. I showed him how much we were paying in interest and he was shocked. We paid off the mortgage and began paying the credit cards in full when they came due. We actually put $7000 a month back into our pockets. He was astounded.

I learned early in my adult life not to pay interest. When I decided that I was not going to work for a company, but rather be self-employed, I knew I had to become adept at handling finance.

I went back to college and took business management and finance. Do you know that you can make an extra payment on the principle (no interest included in that payment) on your mortgage each month and pay that debt within a few years instead of paying interest for thirty years?

So often we forget to thank the people who teach us the grandest lessons—"that which we should not do." My aunt did this for me. She would load up her credit accounts until it became difficult to make the payments. Then she would consolidate all her bills into one easy payment. She never considered how much she was paying in interest. She thought she was being a good manager. The scripture says, "Be careful over a few things and I will make you ruler over many things."

You might ask, "But how do I get out of debt once I have overloaded my accounts?"

First you get rid of the credit cards. You stop buying anything that is not an absolute necessity. You make a goal to be debt-free by a certain date and work toward that goal before you purchase anything. Cut down on everything that contributes to your expense.

Wear the clothes that you already have. Watch TV instead of going to the dinner theaters. Never ever get cash on your credit card.

You will pay the full interest rate from the day you withdraw that money. There is no 28 to 30 days grace before you are charged. Plan your vacation in your own area instead of cruises or expensive trips. Learn to enjoy your home.

When you must do errands, think ahead and do all that are in the same direction so you do not make unnecessary trips. Drive your car for several years instead of trading it in every other year. Most of the millionaires I have known would not think of buying a brand new car. They let someone else take the several thousand dollars depreciation after it is driven only a few miles. Watch for bargains. Pay your tithe. All these things are important.

Never let a check bounce. Not only is it expensive; it can ruin your credit standing for years to come. As you get into a favorable credit situation, begin to think of investing something. Your Social Security will not be sufficient when you retire.

You will need extra income. Set up an IRA or a 401-K. And you might think of annuities for a very safe investment. Learn to be responsible for the management of your funds. If you can't handle money, your future will be very volatile.

How many times do we read where someone won the lottery and within two to three years, they are broke. They have not learned how to handle wealth, so how can God trust them with more.

We have all heard the adage, "A penny saved is a penny earned." Take time to consider how you can save money. Are you thinking of renovating? If so, here are some helpful savings I might suggest. The secret of cost-efficient renovation on your home is knowing where to be thrifty. If you plan to live in that home at least ten years, renovate according to your taste. But if you might move within ten years, it is safer to go for a classic look. If you are not sure whether the people who might purchase your home in a few years would like it, don't use it.

Suppose your kitchen cabinets need refurbishing. The first thought is probably to have a company come in and install new cabinets. You could save thousands of dollars if you have them refaced. If they are basically sound, you could have new doors, counter tops and different knobs and faucets.

Realize that the stylish knobs and faucets will give your kitchen a whole new look and they cost only a little more than the plain ones. But your first dollars should go toward replacing old pipes and wiring. Think of the infrastructure.

Problems that surface after your renovation could force a costly "renovation of your renovation."

If you need to replace an appliance, buy mid-range major appliances. The difference between medium and high price ovens and refrigerators can be a savings of thousands of dollars with only a marginal improvement in quality and looks.

Inexpensive fluorescent lights are easy to install under the cabinets. To improve the lighting in your kitchen, add a four inch trim to hide the under-cabinet light fixtures. These are just a few things to get you thinking of how you can save on expenses.

Guard your possessions. Be very prudent when throwing out your trash. Thieves search through trash to find evidence of credit cards, bank accounts and such. This is how they steal your identity. Minimize the amount of information a thief can steal. Shred or tear off your addresses on incoming mail and personal information. Give heed to the old adage, "An ounce of prevention is worth a pound of cure."

The prophecy, referring to the end times, which most of us feel is near, promises wealth to those who can handle it. Scripture tells us that the wealth will be taken from those who have misused it and shall be given to those who have learned how to use it to help themselves and others.

As prosperity conscious beings we should bless every good thing in our life. What is blessed is yours forever; damn a thing and it will flee from you. Have you noticed that things which are loved and blessed seem to show their respect. Your car will be more accident prone and need repair much more often if you do not love and bless it.

An experiment was conducted where a bed of flowers was divided down the middle. One half was loved and blessed while the other half was cursed. Those blessed ones grew and blossomed and were a delight. The others shriveled up and died. It was found that babies who were held and loved were much healthier.

A good example of this was demonstrated by a friend. She and her husband bought a new Lincoln automobile. And from the day they purchased that car, they found fault with it. She told me that they both hated that car. I wasn't too surprised one day as she related how the car attacked her husband. She said that, as he parked the car and went to get out, the door swung open, knocking him to the ground and then almost rolled over him. "I swear that car attacked him," she declared.

"No wonder," I said, "you have done nothing but curse that car from the day you brought it home."

If you bless your money, it will multiply, and if you curse it, it will indeed flee from you. Respect your money. When placing your paper money in your billfold, turn it all the same way, and don't place them upside-down. Show respect for everything in your life. Hang up your clothes when you undress. Keep your environment neat. Bless all things and all people.

To bless means to wish total, unconditional, unrestricted good for others and events. It must come from the deepest wellspring in the innermost chamber of your heart. It means to hallow, to hold in reverence, to behold with utter awe that which is always a gift from the creator.

This is why we should bless our day. See it as full of unseen good that awaits us from the universe. Trials are blessings in disguise, and hosts of angels follow in their path.

Bless those you pass on the street. When you hear the siren of an emergency vehicle, bless the one who is in need of their service and bless the ones who are going to help. Bless the one who might be in danger, like the child on a bicycle, or motorcycle or someone on foot. Place a cylinder of light around them.

As a candidate for wealth, you must realize that time is your most precious commodity.

Someone said, "Yesterday is gone and I can do nothing about it. Tomorrow never comes, so I am responsible only for today."

Another way to say this: "Yesterday is a canceled check. Tomorrow is a promissory note. Today is legal tender, but only this moment is negotiable."

Learn to live in the moment. Most of our mistakes are born out of trying to live in the future or remembering the mistakes of the past. Scripture says, "Think not of what you will wear tomorrow or what you shall eat or where you will lay your head. Consider the lilies of the field; they toil not nor do they spin, yet Solomon in all his glory was not arrayed like one of these."

And again scripture says that even the very hairs of our head are numbered. Jesus said, "Not one sparrow falls to the ground that the Father doesn't see. How much more precious are you to the Father than one of these?"

If all inhabitants of the world would realize how precious all of us are to God, would we not treat our brothers and sisters with more respect? Jesus said, "As you have done unto these my little ones, you have done it unto me," and this also refers to the way you treat yourself, for you are one of His little ones.

A client, who suffered from low self-esteem, confided in me that she felt that she was not worthy of a certain position that was offered to her. I asked her if she thought Jesus was good enough for such a job. "Of course, but why would you ask me such a thing?"

"Do you know you are one of His little ones?" I asked.

She answered that she does believe that. I said, "He said as you have done to one of these, my little ones, you have done it unto me."

She exclaimed, "Oh, I didn't know that. I swear I will never belittle myself ever again."

Everything affects your ability to stay on top and demonstrate wealth, for being rich is not just money. It is feeling wealthy, feeling good about yourself, feeling good about your neighbors, and being on good terms with the Creator.

You must clear your mind of every dark or disparaging thought or feeling. I have a formula for getting rid of a dark thought or feeling. Often that depressed feeling is not your own but is really coming to you from someone else. It could be from someone who is jealous of you. It could be from someone who loves you and hasn't learned that to worry about you can hurt you.

Or it could be you are more clairvoyant than you realize, and you just picked up the dark thought from someone else.

Many businesses and inventions are not the product of the mind of the thinker. He/she thought about it, therefore putting it into the ethers, but did not have the courage to pursue it, so you or some inventor or entrepreneur picked it out of the ethers and produced the product or business.

Our thoughts are much like radio waves. They are not just wisps of vapor which are dissipated into mid-air. Others can and do pick up our thoughts. It is imperative that if a dark thought or feeling is evident, you rid yourself of it immediately. Here is the formula.

Send a white light in the direction of the feeling, and say this affirmation, "I behold the Christ in you."

You might ask how you will know the direction? You will, believe me. If you get quiet and listen, you will sense not only the direction of the feeling, but you might even see (in your mind's eye) the person. I can focus on the feeling and know who it is coming from.

As you send the light, you will actually feel the burden lifted. What if the dark feeling was coming from your own dark side and you did not realize it? Send the white light anyway.

Everything we send out is like a boomerang and returns to the sender. If it is coming from your dark side, you will receive the blessing yourself.

Jesus taught us to love ourselves and one another. I saw a statement in a magazine along with a picture of an angel. The caption went like this: "We are all angels with but one wing, and only by embracing each other can we fly."

We are all learning that we are one, which is why collective faith has such power. Chants and mantras have worked extremely well for centuries. And Jesus said, "Where two or more are gathered together, I will be in their midst."

Jesse Duplantis, a TV minister, was perturbed with his friend. He was telling his friend about the new jet plane he had just purchased. The friend asked, "Then why are you so perturbed with me? You got your plane, didn't you?"

Jesse replied, "Yes, but it took five years. All I ever asked of you was to have faith with me that I could have that plane. I didn't ask you for money or any of your time, just your faith.

You didn't believe me, so it took me five years to realize my dream. If you had applied your faith with mine, I wouldn't have had to wait five years. I could have had it immediately."

It is important not to share your dreams with anyone who might doubt them for they could hold back your progress. Share your goal only with those who can and will have faith with you.

Our Heavenly Father wants two things from you: your appreciation and for you to be happy with the blessings He brings into your life. I can't find in the scripture that you will be blessed if you go around with a long face. But I can find numerous scriptures that promise that, if you will stay happy, you can have anything your heart desires. The Bible says, "Make a joyful noise unto the Lord." And again it states, " I will give you the desires of your heart."

Do you know how much good a laugh does for you? The Mayo Clinic teaches that laughter aids breathing. It also helps many functions of the body such as clearing mucous from the lungs. It increases circulation and improves the delivery of oxygen and nutrients to the tissues throughout your body. Laughter helps your immune system fight off colds and flu. Norman Cousins used to say that laughter is so beneficial that it is like "inner jogging."

Laughter is good for the heart and is a good stress reliever. It raises the level of endorphins and can even help control pain. I read that a child on the average, laughs four hundred times a day.

Adults just do not laugh as much as children. Why not? Laughter makes you feel great and is so good for you. Solomon said, "Laughter doeth good like a medicine, but a frown dries up the bones."

Laughter is completely organic. It can be shared and recycled and is absolutely free. If you always face the sun, you will never see shadows.

Dale Carnegie gives us five motivators that will aid us in our search for success and wealth. (1) Build great self-confidence. (2) Strengthen people skills. (3) Enhance communication skills. (4) Develop leadership skills. (5) Control worry and stress.

We accomplish little until we are confident that we measure up to our own highest ideals. First, love God. The golden rule is a good way to get started: Do unto others as you would have others do unto you. Then love your neighbor as yourself. Forgiveness is one of the next best foundations to build on. That means, forgive yourself as well as others.

The way you feel about yourself and money can make or break you. When you no longer love money, but rather love the things money can do, then money is no longer a problem.

The Bible does not say that money is the root of all evil. It says that the love of money is the root of all evil. Concentrate on receiving money for the good that you can do with it. Having a prosperity consciousness will solve your money problems. Jesus summed it up this way. Know (have faith) that all your needs are met, according to His Father's riches in glory. He said, "If you had faith as a grain of mustard seed, you could remove mountains"—mountains of debt, mountains of unworthiness, mountains of fear and need.

Having low self-esteem is one of the worst things you can do to yourself. Jesus says that we are joint heirs with him. Then how can you be unworthy? Do you know that God loves you so much that He has appointed a legion of angels to take care of your needs? A legion is six thousand angels, just for you.

We must first learn to love ourselves before we can properly love anyone else. Realize that it is very wrong to look down on yourself. God is not happy with us when we belittle ourselves. We must take time to nurture ourselves. Mothers, especially, become so involved in looking out for the needs of the family that they forget that mothers should count, too. Often we, as mothers, begin to feel more like servants than as favored children of God. It is difficult to even feel that we are deserving of giving time to ourselves.

I remember a class I attended that stressed the importance of loving one's self. Our assignment at the end of a particular class was that we were to spend a whole week doing only whatever we wanted: to think of ourselves first. She said, "If you don't feel like getting up, don't. If you feel like having breakfast in bed, do so. Do whatever makes you happy. Learn to love yourself. Make time for you." That was one of the most fulfilling weeks I can remember.

Try this for a week. Go to bed thirty minutes early—you will wake up feeling refreshed. Meditate for ten minutes before getting out of bed. Eat a leisurely breakfast. Exercise for thirty minutes. Read ten pages of a good book. Buy fresh flowers so you wake up to beautiful sights and fragrances. If this list isn't just right for you, make up your own list based on your needs. Your body and spirit will show its appreciation. This is a first step in learning to nurture yourself.

Don't become discouraged if you make a mistake. They are bound to happen. Keep mistakes in perspective. Regard them not as failures but rather as part of the learning process.

When great tennis players are training, they hit a large percentage of the balls into the net and out of bounds. They aren't failing. They are practicing.

A good sales person knows he/she must make an average of eight calls before making a sale. When he gets turned down, he doesn't consider it as personal. He knows he hasn't lost a sale, he is just another step closer to achieving his goal. He must have no fear of attempting another sale. Remember Franklin D. Roosevelt said, "Do the thing you fear and the death of fear is certain."

Many times the reason we are in lack is because we forget to ask or feel too unworthy to ask. He said, "Ask and it shall be given you, seek and you shall find, knock and it shall be opened unto you."

And in another scripture, it says, "You receive not because you ask not. Ask that your joy may be full."

Often we would rather just let God take care of it. This is the easy way out, of not having to make a decision. But remember, He takes into consideration that He gave us free will and, if we want to do things the hard way, we may. We must take the responsibility by asking.

Don't just take it for granted that your angels, who are assigned to you, will handle it.

They cannot override your free will. But if you ask them, they are obliged to do whatever you ask.

I hear so often, "But, isn't it selfish to ask for money or really big things?" The answer is, "Absolutely not." The fact that you can desire a thing is evidence you should have it. The only requisite is that you hurt no one in getting what you want.

Hurt no one, means also, yourself. God loves a happy person. If having riches will make you a more loving, happier person, then go for it. You can do far more good with money than you can without it.

One main requisite to becoming wealthy is to clear your mind of all obstacles. To make your life easier so you can concentrate on becoming wealthy, use the trinity number of three. Identify the three most important things you need to accomplish. Focus on these three until they are completed and out of the way. If there is something you are dreading, do it now. Don't let it sit there and fester. Get it out of the way.

Set one certain day to do the administrative chores. Don't think of the things that may not bring results. Focus on the more important activities. Rather than checking the e-mail several times a day, plan one day to answer all e-mail. Learn to say "no."

One of the reasons we get overloaded is that we keep saying yes to new projects no matter how busy we are. Clean your plate before adding anything new. Realize that you count, too.

If you have ever thought of the possibility of bankruptcy, please put that out of your mind. It will follow you all your life. Having a good credit reference is one of the best things you should strive for.

But if you have already made that step and taken bankruptcy, do not despair. There are many organizations who will help you clear your name. There are some banks and other organizations who will offer a counseling service at low fees to help you get back to a "good risk" situation. They will look at the money coming in and going out each month and help you control unnecessary spending. They will teach you budget, debt and credit management.

If it is your dream to own your own home, having a good credit report will be essential. Quite often potential employers, insurance agencies, and landlords use these reports to determine if you are a good risk.

It is important that you know what your credit report reveals. If you have applied for credit or employment and have been turned down, you are entitled to a free copy of the report.

CHAPTER FIFTEEN

Ask That Your Joy May Be Full

Having control of your life and finances is a sure-fire way of easing your mind so you can go on to important things like setting a goal for financial freedom. If you will set that goal, your angels will be there to guide you all the way.

I often have people ask, "Is it all right to ask your angels and guides for little things?"

Of course it is. Angels and guides want to elevate their status just as much as you do yours. Since they are assigned to you, the only way they can do this is for you to give them things to do. I ask for many small things. As an example, one day I wanted to color my hair but found that I had no hair color.

I looked in the cabinet where I always keep it and even had my husband look also, but there was none. Finally I said to my angel, "For goodness sake, you could materialize one bottle!"

My little voice said, "Look again." I did; and right where my husband and I had looked over and over, there in plain view was one bottle. I said, "Thank you, Angel, I only needed one."

I'll tell you about one of my guides called, General Tumnik. I call him "General" because he is in charge of things in general. He is Turkish and wears a stone in the middle of his forehead in his third eye. He sits tailor-fashion in mid-air. He was revealed to me by a psychic lady. I have gotten to know him well.

I have had students ask me if it is all right to accept a guide or angel that was revealed to them through a psychic. I tell them, "Certainly, that is how I met General Tumnik."

One day I had a call from my publisher. He was going to be on the east coast of Florida and since we live on the west coast, he wanted us to pay him a visit at a hotel where he was making an appearance.

My husband and I are not familiar with that particular area and we got lost. We were about to be late and we had no idea where we were. Finally I said, "Tumnik, where in the world are you? You are supposed to be in charge here."

At that moment my husband swung the car into an alley. I said, "Why in the world did you do a thing like that? Aren't we lost enough as it is? Furthermore we are going to be late."

Not caring too much for my brashness, Lou encountered, "I just felt like doing it. That's why!"

It turned out to be short-cut to the hotel. I said, "Thank you, Tumnik. You are always there when we need you."

Doesn't it make you feel really blessed to know that God loves you so much that he assigns angels just to do things for you? If you have an angel encounter, don't question it; just be thankful and respond to it.

Learn to respond rather than to react. The wise person responds to any need, his own or someone else's. But he never reacts to what another does or says. That is not his responsibility. To react to another is giving away your power. The wise person considers a rebuke the other person's problem.

Look for positive solutions to every problem. Believe there is always another option. Be optimistic. This attitude enables you to find solutions that you might not ever have thought of. Optimism and creativity will make you a winner every time.

Be quick to forgive and allow yourself to make excuses for the other person. Go about your day as if you have all the answers, for you really do. But if you get upset, you close off your channel. That channel must be kept open for your angels to come through.

Do you know that angels respond to color and sound? I was instructed by one of my guides that when I want to write, to visualize all different colors around me. First pink, the color of love. Then blue, which comes from Archangel Michael. It signifies, "Thy will be done."

Then yellow, the color of inspiration. Next, green for healing and growth; and lavender to help us understand our divine nature. When I sit down at my computer, I get very quiet and do my visualization.

Almost immediately my angels are at my side, helping me. It doesn't have to be just writing; they will respond to these colors to help you with any problem you might have.

You might wonder what all this has to do with becoming wealthy. It is all very important to make you receptive to receiving riches.

Get all of the obstacles out of the way so prosperity can flow to you. When you don't know what to do, pray for wisdom, counsel, understanding, knowledge and right judgment.

Take responsibility for the consequences of your own life. No one is responsible for them but you. Refusing to be a victim gives you great liberty. Learn to set goals—both short and long term. If you say, "I want lots of money and a beautiful house and a wonderful mate," that is not a goal. You are speaking in generalities. Goals must be specific.

You must know how much money you desire by a specific date. You need to know what that dream house looks like, even have an idea how it will feel to live there. When it comes to a mate, don't settle for just anyone. Ask for one who will love you and who possesses the attributes you would most admire in a partner, who loves the things you love, who has the same high ideals that are important to you.

I'd like to share an affirmation that my husband and I use in our daily meditation/prayer session. It is an affirmation for prosperity and your divine, right work: "The spirit of truth within me is guiding me to my divine right work. Through this work I give and receive blessings. I love my work and my work loves me.

"Every door is open and my way is made clear. I know what to do and I do it. Everyone is prospered by the service I am called to provide. I love to serve. I serve with joyous abandon for the simple joy of serving. My prosperity is assured. God's rich abundance flows in a steady, ever increasing stream of plenty into and through my life. I always have more than enough to share with all. Thank you, God. God is my Source." Say this affirmatively morning and night, knowing that it is so.

Have you ever wondered why sometimes your faith pays off and other times things didn't happen as you believed they would? It is because your faith wavered or it was to your best advantage not to have it happen at that particular time. This is where we might have to apply the rule, "Let go, and let God."

But more often it is because we believed in defeat more than we believed in victory. As an example, let's say you are being taught to play a certain game. Why is it that you are such a whiz at this game? Most often you will defeat the champion, at first. I've had this happen in my own life. The reason is that you are being taught only one thing: how to win at this game. You haven't learned how to lose. No one taught you that, so you do the only thing possible (as far as your mind is concerned) ... you win.

But what happened as you got into competition in this game? Someone has to lose. There can be only one winner. Now, you have seen someone lose at this game, so you start losing. Why?

You had not experienced a loss, yours or someone else's until now. But now you have seen the picture of how to lose. It is synonymous with your young son who hits a home run every time at bat until he sees someone lose. What happens? He remembers and he strikes out because he saw the picture of losing.

This is how our mind works—remember the session earlier where we talk about how the mind must materialize the picture? What can we do? Change the picture to what you want to manifest in your life. Never, never think of what you do not want!!!

If your child fails at something or strikes out at bat, this is a good time to brainstorm strategies with him/her by encouraging imaginative thinking.

Having a strategy is one of the best pathways to achieving goals—not only for your child but for you, as well. Set your goal so it is attainable and realistic.

Many times I am asked in Treasure-mapping class if it is all right to entreat for a relative to leave him/her a fortune. I answer this way, "Why narrow God's path to fulfilling your goal by one method. Set your goal for a certain amount of money by a particular date."

God has millions, possibly billions of ways to fulfill your goal. This is why you never try to figure out where the answer to your dream is coming from. Your province is setting the goal."

In a recent discussion, a friend informed me that she had just quit her job. She said, "It seemed that my employer was belittling my position and I felt like I was above that!"

The very next day she was offered another job, closer to her home with chances of an elevated position. I laughed and told her she just got kicked upstairs. She felt good that she was not afraid to step out and do what her consciousness told her.

Have you ever asked yourself, "What are my most dominant fears?" We know fear is debilitating. I was surprised as one lady told me she was "scared to death" of dying. I tried to assure her that I had died and that indeed it was the most wonderful experience.

If you have lost a loved one, just know that he/she is still alive. They just vacated a worn-out house: their body. Since we are Spirit and the body is the house we inhabit, when one dies, they are still alive. Look at what happens to that body when the spirit leaves. It no longer functions. It is just a dead piece of meat. There are instances where the spirit was photographed as it left the body.

We really do not die. Nothing on earth is dead. Everything is alive. Our bodies are constantly regenerating. Our cells were created with the ability to regenerate forever. Many factors contribute to this ability to regenerate. The most powerful is your perception of what it means to regenerate. Your body will follow that formula. Deepak Chopra writes extensively about this. He says that our cells are eavesdropping on our every thought. And since the cells have the same intelligence as we, they see that it happens as we perceive it.

Our perception is the way we view things. I believe that most of us who are alive now will not ever go through the process called death. We will ascend into the fifth dimension.

We know that, at the molecular level, our cells are now being programmed by the Angelic Hierarchy for a light body, and our vibrations are being accelerated to accommodate the frequency of the increased vibrations of Planet Earth. Since Earth will be ascending into the fifth dimension, we must be ready to do the same. Even as we strive to live life to the fullest, we must stick to our highest resolution: to experiencing heaven whether here on earth or in that fifth dimension.

Another important lesson we must learn to achieve wealth and peace of mind is to understand the law of non-resistance. This may not sound like a positive means for achieving wealth, but it is a very important one. Jesus said it this way, "Resist not evil." Deepak Chopra says it like this, "When we put up no defense, there is nothing left to attack."

This premise was viewed earlier in this book when we stated that an evolved person does not react to what another does or says. He knows that is the other person's problem.

If something that another says, hurts, it is probably because it is true. Think about why it stings and learn a lesson from it.

Look at the way we usually think. When we set up a goal, what happens? Our negative programming sets in and we begin to think, "What defenses must I initiate to make sure I reach my goal."

We immediately think of all the things that can go wrong, thereby setting up obstacles.

These prevent us from achieving that goal. We set up our own barriers. We make our own problems. Remember! If you do not think about it, it can't possibly happen.

I'll give you an example. You get in the car to go somewhere. If you are talking to someone about anything other than the trip, you have no problems with the traffic lights or a parking place or the traffic. All goes well. But if you are alone and your old programming sets in, you begin to think about the traffic. You picture the red lights and the parking place and the difficulties begin. Why? You thought about it negatively. You formed a picture in your mind.

I have a formula for when you are in a hurry: Do not think of the traffic, the lights, etc. Project your thoughts to your destination. See yourself in that store making a purchase. This way you don't set up obstacles. See how it works! We must stay positive.

We are all magnetic poles and we attract the people and situations in accordance with our thinking. If we are positive, we attract positive persons and circumstances, and if we are negative, we attract the opposite. We are all accountable for what we create, but no matter what we create, we can overcome. We are not our feelings nor our circumstances.

We are much more. We must value and respect our own body as well as the body of others. Our mind can be our best friend or our worst enemy. Dr. Epstein's book, *Visualization to Mortality,* tells us that the mind and body are inseparable ... that we have always been a mind-body machine. He told a patient who had prostate cancer to go inside his body and find where the trouble area was and to fix it. He was urged to use his imagination.

Learning the proper relaxing technique, he followed the doctor's advice and went inside his body. He actually found the area and destroyed the cancer with his mind. Then he burned all the papers of his diagnosis and the cancer was gone. Healing can take many avenues. But have you considered the fact that sometimes it is not only the body that needs healing. Sometimes a situation or an emotion or a state of mind needs healing. A dispute with your mate can need healing. Healing through the mind by visualization really works.

So, if you have anything that needs healing, use your visualization techniques and take care of it. You might ask, "How do I do this?" First think of how you are picturing that problem right now. Are you seeing the lack of money in your bank account? What would be the opposite of that picture?

Think of what it would be like to have all the money you need. What would you buy with it? Who might you share it with? What debts would you eliminate? Where would you pay your tithe? Any one of these pictures will heal that lack in your life, if you can really believe it. You can use this technique for every problem in your life. Just place the correct picture in your mind. Realize how powerful your mind is.

To become prosperity conscious you must look at money as a form of energy, and knowing that like attracts like, since you are energy, money wants to come to you.

You have been misinformed to believe that you must work hard or be born with money to manifest wealth. You must invite prosperity into your life. Once you build an openness to receiving money, it is then free to flow to you. This is the law of attraction which is basic for our Planet.

You must negate all the old beliefs that it is hard to attract money. Then you will be free to receive it. And you must never envy those who are wealthy. It is important for you to feel that you are worthy of achieving prosperity. Your fear of not having enough will only set up more barriers to prevent you from receiving wealth. If you will become open and receptive, prosperity will find you. It is a natural law.

CHAPTER SIXTEEN

Remove the Barriers

It is imperative that you remove all hindrances to your prosperity consciousness. If you have had to set up barriers (defenses) in order not to be hurt, they must be removed.

A good example is if you had a difficult time as a child; maybe someone made fun of you, a friend betrayed you, or you didn't receive the love and understanding from a parent you felt you needed. You may have set up barriers that you did not realize existed. These defenses have prevented you from receiving the good God had in store for you all your life.

Even though you put up these barriers to protect yourself from being hurt, these barriers are an obstacle. In order to keep you from being hurt, they also kept you from receiving love, wealth and the very things you were striving for.

A client who very much wanted to have a strong angel presence in her life recently learned a lesson about how we block the things that are most important to us.

She felt an angel communication and had a few miracles as a result, but she wanted to feel their presence as a strong love influence. Through counseling, she learned that she had built up a strong barrier due to her marriage to an undemonstrative mate. She felt that if she flung her heart open to love him, she could be hurt because he would not respond in kind.

She had lived with these defenses for so long she did not know they existed. After her husband's demise, she needed that demonstration of love from her angels more than ever.

She called on them and they responded. For instance, I advised her to light a candle and go through every room in her house to dedicate her home to God. As she walked through each room with her candle in hand, dedicating each room and bringing in the light to remove all negative influences, she felt the angel presence so close.

The candle in her hand began to shift from one side to the other. She could tell it was not of her own volition. The angel presence which she had desperately desired was so overwhelming she had to go lie down.

Another time her angels took her shopping. She was one of these people that would never think of herself; she was too busy taking care of everyone but herself.

She was in a shopping mall on the ground floor when suddenly she found herself on an upper floor in the ladies' department. She did not know how she got there. But suddenly, completely out of character, she began to purchase everything in sight. She came home with her arms full of gifts for herself. She was baffled as to how she could have had so much fun, doing this for herself.

I told her that her angels were teaching her that she must learn to nurture herself. She said, "I knew it had to be someone besides me because I don't even know how I got to the upper floor, and I normally would never buy things for myself except the bare necessities."

These were wonderful angel demonstrations, but she needed love more than anything else after the loss of her husband. She began to follow my advice and asked her angels to help her remove the barriers that she had built up over the years.

They responded in kind and today she has a wonderful family of angels. They are always close and she has never felt such love as they express daily. She never feels alone.

Now that the barriers have come down, her path is clear for prosperity and all the good things to flow into her life. Notice I said, "flow" not "strive for." Prosperity flows if we do not put up obstacles to deter it.

Another obstacle to prosperity consciousness comes to mind. If you were brought up in a certain religious belief that you are a worm of the dust, that you should be content with meager provisions, you already have a defense against ever becoming wealthy unless you can convince yourself otherwise.

You can do this by searching the scriptures. You will find that you are indeed worthy of every good thing. We deserve all the good that God wishes to provide us. Knowing that all good is from God, how can we throw his blessings back in His face?

One associate had kept himself from riches because he read in the Bible, "It is easier for a camel to go through the eye of the needle than for a rich man to enter heaven."

It was resolved for him when I explained that "The Eye of the Needle" was a gate in the countries that use camels as beasts of burden. The gate was so low that for a camel to go through that gate, it was necessary to unload the burden from the camel's back and then for the camel to get down on his knees and literally crawl through.

Here is the meaning: in order for a rich man to go to heaven, he must unload his burdens (the things that are keeping him from being spiritual) and must be humble, humble enough to get on his knees if necessary.

In other words the rich man must do whatever it takes to have God in his life and he can go to heaven. Earlier in this book we talk of the scripture that says, "The love of money is the root of all evil." Money is divine as is every other thing God made.

Don't ever refer to money as filthy lucre or in any other disrespectful manner. But if you so love money and riches that you will do anything to get it, even to hurting yourself or others to have it, that is where the evil lies. The rich man must not allow his money to control him.

Learning to control the mind is paramount in clearing the way for good health, prosperity and fulfillment to manifest in your life. The basic requirement for controlling your mind is taking charge of your thoughts. Discard the belief that our thoughts are automatic, that we can do nothing about them.

Thoughts are not just wisps of vapor that go out into the universe to be dissipated. Indeed we are responsible for our every thought. Thoughts are actually vibrations that affect others and the universe. Some scientists say that the vibrations resulting from collective negative thoughts are what cause tornadoes, earthquakes and many different kinds of disasters.

If we can learn to control our mind and our thoughts, we can control our world. Here are some ideas for doing that. First, we must relax the body in order to control the mind. Have you ever tried lying down when you are angry? It is nearly impossible to be furious while in a reclining position.

So, we need relaxation of the body as well as the mind. An altered state of consciousness, the "theta" mind state, is most important.

And it is next to impossible to think of anything negative while in the "theta" brain wave frequency. I recommend using a cyber-optic poster, sometimes referred to as a "theta-gram," like the one pictured in my book *Metaphysical Techniques That Really Work* on page 49, as an aid for getting into the theta brain wave frequency.

My husband and I use a theta-gram during our meditation. It is impossible to get into "theta-land" if you are not completely relaxed. In this altered state of mind you open yourself up to greater abundance and opportunity. In this theta brain wave frequency you are 95% more effective than when in your work-a-day-world mind state.

Yoga is another good method for controlling the mind. When we bring our body under control, it is much easier to control the mind. This is very well demonstrated by the fire-walking yogis who walk on a bed of hot coals at temperatures that should have reduced their feet to smoldering stumps, yet at the end of the walk they suffer not so much as a blister.

In controlling the mind we are no longer preoccupied with the past, or fearful of the future.

We know that "the now" will lead us to making the present moment vibrant and alive, and we are fulfilling the most important function in the universe.

We no longer contribute to the energy of the dark forces but rather we look for every opportunity to change that darkness into light. It is better to light one little candle than to curse the darkness.

A beautiful prayer that addresses this situation is the AA prayer, "Lord, grant me the courage to change the things I can, the serenity to accept the things I cannot change, and the wisdom to know the difference."

If you are worried about anything at this moment, stop and ask yourself, "How will I feel about this five years from now?"

You probably won't even remember what you were worried about, or if you do, you will see it in a whole new light. It is like reading a favorite book. If you lay that book aside for five years and then read it again, it will not have the same meaning it had previously. You know the book hasn't changed. You have.

We are constantly changing. Since our thoughts do go out into the universe, we must be ever diligent about their content.

Controlling your mind and your thoughts will illumine in you a new vision of yourself and your role in the universe. It will show you that you are much more than you ever imagined. As you meditate on the enormous potential of your mind, it awakens you to a joyful experience, one without fear or guilt and certainly without judgment.

If we could see the actual picture, we would see a virtual paradise of abundance. Just think: every day we are offered beauty, opportunity, ability, even ingenuity, and we can decide to what extent we wish to indulge ourselves in them. Jesus said, "I came that you might have life and have it more abundantly."

Another scripture, Mt. 6:33 says, "But strive first for the kingdom of God and His righteousness, and all these things will be added." Of course Jesus wasn't speaking of only physical things. He was meaning that we are as rich as we will decide to be; that if we open ourselves to the beauty and opportunities that are available to us, we can have it all. I read that every five years each person is given an opportunity to become wealthy. But most of us are so preoccupied that we don't see it and it passes us by.

We are all unique and some of us have degrees to which we are more receptive to the prosperity within and around us.

It seems that in some cases, a person is just not willing to accept the good that is trying to come through to them. The time of day may play a part, or if you are tired or busy. If we allow ourselves to get caught up in the chaos of everyday living, it may hinder us from even seeing the possibilities.

It is as if we need to retrain our eyes. We tend to focus on what is wrong rather than what is right. If we could learn to magnify the good in our lives as completely as we magnify the things that go wrong, what a world this would be! We need to be willing to make prosperity consciousness and joy a priority in our life. It would be wise to have a journal where you jot down every good thing that happens in your life. And then take time to read it often; learn to praise your Creator for being able to see, for the ability to walk, to eat delicious food, to enjoy the flowers and trees, a blue sky, a sunny day, a warm bed, a home, friends and companions. The list is endless.

When a friend does a good deed for you, magnify it by asking a blessing for that person and add to it an affirmation such as, "Everyone wants to help me." When unexpected money comes to you, say, "Wealth is on its way. It is seeking me."

Do an unexpected good deed, like paying for the toll for the person behind you when traveling.

You will be blessed for every good deed. My husband and I missed our chance for a blessing one day as we arrived at the mall. We were finding a place to park when we saw a lady who looked like she was down on her luck. By the time we got parked, she was gone. We looked for her but never found her. This taught us a good lesson.

We wanted to help her not for the blessing we would receive so much as to just be there for someone in need. Though we must expect a blessing for each good deed, for that is the law. We took envelopes and put some money in them for a bus ticket and information telling the recipient where there was shelter and a meal. We don't want to get caught unprepared again.

Oh, if only we had been taught to expect a blessing for the good we do when we were small, the world would be a better place for it. Wouldn't it be great if parents, schools and especially newspapers would lecture us on success formulas and teach us to be ready for the many blessings that could confront us at every turn.

Instead we are taught how to handle disasters; be ready to face failure, make ready for the rainy day. Wouldn't it be great if schools and parents would teach us how to deal with prosperity, successful endeavors and maintenance of happy relationships, fulfilling careers, the wonder of a loving mate and parenthood?

If magazines, billboards, TV and internet would focus on the positive rather than the negative, it would change our world.

We are "God in expression." Charles Fillmore, the founder of the Unity movement said, "All the ideas contained in one Father-Mind are at the mental command of its offspring. Get behind a thing into the mental realm where it exists as an inexhaustible idea, and you can draw upon it and never deplete the source."

To be prosperity conscious we must refuse to get involved in casual conversation about the terrible economy, the high cost of living, or anything you would not like to manifest in our world. Refuse to even joke about it. Words are things—they materialize.

Stay in the creative flow. Keep moving in the direction of your goals. Know that you are surrounded by a divine presence that wishes for you only good and realize that God will help you bring your dreams to fruition if you will just be willing. A good affirmation to use every morning and night is, "God is my instant, constant, and abundant source of supply."

God loves a cheerful giver. If you cannot give with joy, don't give. This applies to tithing and your time as well as gifts. Here are some gifts that don't cost you a thing, but which enrich the life of the giver as well as the receiver.

GIVE GIFTS THAT COST YOU NOTHING

Give the gift of listening. No interrupting, no daydreaming, no planning your response. Just listen. I knew a lady who would talk incessantly. She missed so much, for she was so busy thinking of how she was going to respond that she never heard a word of the speaker.

Give the gift of affection. Be generous with appropriate hugs, kisses and pats on the back and hand-holds. If I think a lovely thought of someone but never actually reveal it to the person, we both lose. A touch can mean so much. I recall a lovely sentiment, "Reach out and touch someone, today."

Give the gift of laughter. Clip cartoons. Save funny stories. Your gift will say, "I love to laugh with you." Laughter builds endorphins which can actually heal the body. If you feel you do not laugh enough, call on your "joy guide." You surely have one. Mine is named "Giva." When I feel I am getting too serious, I call on Giva and I have found myself laughing at things that at other times I would not consider funny.

Give the gift of a written note. It can be a simple "thank you" or a full sonnet. A brief, handwritten message may be remembered for a lifetime and may even change a life. My sister would much rather get a handwritten letter from me than my computer driven letters, even though I can cram much more into them. At special times I try to take time to write to her in long hand.

Give the gift of a favor. Every day, go out of your way to do something kind for someone. Try this. It really is a fulfilling venture. Make an effort to find someone to do something special for. It will bless your life far more than it does the recipient.

Give the gift of a cheerful disposition. The easiest way to feel good is to extend a kind word to someone. It really is not that hard to say "Hello" or "Thank you." There are people who live alone and never have the pleasure of saying one word to anyone. This is why they walk the malls and sometimes take jobs they don't need, just to be where there are people.

I remember reading where a gentleman in New York City was so alone; he said this was so, even in a crowded elevator, that he felt life was not worth living. No one ever spoke to him. He decided to walk over the bridge that spanned the river and he decided that if no one spoke to him, he was going to jump. It happened that a man coming from the other direction said, "Isn't it a lovely morning?" It saved that man's life.

Give the gift of a compliment. A simple and sincere "You look great, today," "You did a super job," or "That was a wonderful meal," can make someone's day. It is so important to care how you say a thing. Make the compliment sound as if you really mean it.

I remember a compliment that changed a woman's life. She was very conscious of her big hands. She constantly tried to hide them. After being married for thirty years, one day her husband said, "Honey, I feel I should tell you the thing I have admired the most about you in all our years of marriage is your hands. They seem so capable of so many things, like soothing a fevered brow, caring for a family, making wonderful meals and are so wonderful to hold."

She had been trying to hide those precious hands for so long, never knowing how he felt. That thought-felt compliment changed her life.

Give the gift of solitude. There are times when we need nothing better than to be left alone. Be sensitive to those times. My dear friend, Helen, lost her husband. His death was devastating. I called and sent letters and prayed for her because I knew she needed her solitude to learn how to deal with such a loss. At times like this we feel as though our hands are tied behind our back, not being able to help.

Give the gift of unconditional love: Loving all the earth and thinking, feeling and doing only what is for the highest and best good of everyone you interact with daily.

Be aware of the tremendous opportunities you possess to bring light where there has been only darkness. Just know that you are capable of sending energy where it is needed.

The human brain emits energy fields resembling structures and processes found in the cosmos. It could be speculated that the brain performs much the same actions as a universe. The ancient Chinese have always believed that the Tao (universe) was in the head. They say that in higher states of consciousness as in deep meditation they experience a radical difference of space-time; that one enters a fourth dimension where space and time are integrated.

Sacred enlightened human beings, such as Jesus and Buddha, had the ability to manipulate the energy of consciousness and co-exist in both realms. A mind that is less evolved has simply not learned the way to use this consciousness to turn off the reality distortion field that surrounds them creating the three-dimensional experience of time and space. A central thesis of sages and mystics long before the so-called New Age movement has been that we live in an illusion.

This seems to imply that our experiences in this third dimension are not real, when indeed life is really happening to us. It might be better explained as a distortion of space-time reality rather than as an illusion. It is well established that in certain altered states of consciousness, there is a profound shift in brainwave frequencies. If you awaken in your alpha brain wave frequency, you will remember your dreams. We drift from beta to alpha to theta all through the night. The subconscious mind, which is synonymous with these altered states, never sleeps.

This is why the theta brain wave frequency is your best tool for getting into your altered state of consciousness. The exploration of these different states through meditation, biofeedback and other modalities seems to bring about an extraordinary acceleration of psychic phenomena and psychological information.

D.T. Suzuki says, "In the spiritual world there are no time divisions as to past, present or future; for they have contracted themselves into a single moment of the present where life quivers in its true sense.

"The past and future are both rolled up in this present moment of illumination, and this present moment is not something standing still with all its contents, for it ceaselessly moves on."

In the new millennium the biggest and most important discoveries will come from the journey within.

Brain research will advance to a completely new level and reveal far reaching secrets about the true nature of our minds.

William Blake, an English poet, experienced visions as a child and went on to produce a body of work describing it. He wrote:

> To see the world in a grain of sand
> And a heaven in a wild flower
> Hold infinity in the palm of your hand
> And eternity in an hour

Time does seem to stand still at times of altered states of consciousness. But I have found that it can happen when one is wide awake. I can think of several occasions when I did not know if a minute, an hour, or days had passed.

LEARN TO USE THE MAGIC OF PYRAMID POWER

The key that unlocks the door to Higher Consciousness is your treasure chest within the unlimited area of your mind. Your altered state of consciousness is that magic realm between awakening and sleep.

I was in a very deep state of consciousness as I slept. I was working with my son and we were into building pyramids. It was so fascinating as I visualized a pyramid over my bed which sent me into an even deeper dream state. The pyramid seemed to have a lot of orange color. I began listening to my heart which told me that I could build an invisible pyramid over my bed, my house, my car, my jacuzzi, and especially over my office.

I began to ask my higher self how? I heard, "Build an invisible Pyramid over your bed right now and see what you feel."

So I did and the experience was astounding. I felt a deep sense of my higher self—that state of being *in* this world but not *of* this world—and yet I was very relaxed as my mind began to build pyramids in many places. It was as though I was wide awake yet I was in a deep state of meditation.

Then that little voice said, "You can sleep under this invisible pyramid and grow younger, receive more vigor and strength, find peace and love and create miracles."

So I placed an invisible pyramid over my bed. It seemed to draw me into a very deep relaxation and yet I was beaming with energy. I could feel myself actually getting much younger and more vigorous. I actually was feeling like a much younger person. I liked that!

Then I remember once when I seemed to be with all my loved ones who had passed on, and my grandmother who died when I was a small child said to me, "Get back to your Pyramid Power!"

I remembered that none of my family had ever mentioned pyramids. I'm sure that none of them had ever given pyramids a single thought.

This experience also triggered a recall of conversations with a man, via email, named Ben Smith (the name has been changed for obvious reasons). He builds great pyramids in many places in the world ... replicas of the great pyramids in Egypt. I began to search my past emails for that record of mine and Ben's emails to each other.

It contained some valuable information which I would like to pass on to you, the reader. One very interesting thing concerned a Pyramid Helmet.

He built it to help bring one into God awareness through Consciousness Meditation, he told me. He also builds very large pyramids which he uses as Star Gates. Ben said that the first pyramid he built was the exact size of the capstone of the Great Pyramid in Egypt. He taught me how one can build their own pyramid, but you must not use metal. He does use aluminum for the base.

This experience also brought me back as I remembered a great man I knew twenty or more years ago. He was one of the wisest men I had ever met. He told me how he made a pyramid of cheese cloth and hung it over his bed. The shape is what gives pyramids their power, not the material they are built from. This, he believed, triggered his great brain power. He gives this pyramid experience credit for his tremendous success.

I learned much from these two great gentlemen. It had been a long time since I even thought of this great pyramid power.

My dream state brought it all back, and I am even now experiencing more youth and vigor than I have known for a very long time. I can still feel that tremendous strength, lifting me up as I visualize that invisible pyramid.

I ask you, the reader, to just try it. I have always taught my students something I learned from Einstein: that the invisible world is the real world. If you can see it, you can do it. Try to see an invisible pyramid over your bed tonight as you doze off to sleep.

My last night's experience was so profound. I asked my Angels to keep that pyramid over my bed from now on. Even now as I sit at my computer, I can visualize that pyramid over my bed, over me and my computer, over my jacuzzi, and over my car as a protecting Angel force.

Nothing happens until someone thinks about it. And note that you cannot think without seeing a picture. It is your Angel's duty to materialize that picture; be it good or bad. Remember Angels were created for man, not the other way around. The thing you think about even in its invisible state is just as real to your Angel as when materialized. This is why my invisible pyramid is so powerful. I plan to use it every night to make me younger, more vigorous and certainly more informed.

If you would like to grow younger, have more energy, or just want to feel great, build an invisible pyramid over your bed and try it out. But you might need a tangible thing like my great friend. Then build it out of some sort of material; just make sure it is not built of metal, whether visible or invisible. If you happen to have the book, *The Reincarnation of Edgar Cayce,* you will find much Pyramid Power information beginning on page 357.

ANOTHER DIMENSION OR WHAT?

These days we hear much about other dimensions, but quite a few years ago, not many were willing to share their miraculous happenings and hardly anyone discussed things like different dimensions. I had heard of a thin veil that gets thinner all the time which separates us from other planets. This miracle happened more than twenty years ago, so that veil or dimension must be extremely thin by now. I never expected to experience any such thing. A friend and I were thrust into another dimension and it was an encounter I will never forget.

I have been a counselor and teacher most of my adult life and my students have always been adults. I must tell you about an adventure my student, Dennis, and I experienced when we went to the fabulous Tiki Restaurant for dinner to celebrate his promotion. This was about the most famous place around and was perfect for such a celebration. The statues, waterfalls and soothing music complemented the occasion. The elegant paintings, palm trees and lush foliage could have been a scene from an island paradise.

The maitre d', waiters in tie and tails, and the waitresses in skimpy French uniforms with ruffled aprons were scurrying about. As usual, the place was crowded. The atmosphere was charged with excitement!

We were anxiously waiting to be served as we enjoyed the out-of-this-world atmosphere when, without warning, either we were thrust into another world or everyone else was.

A hush engulfed the entire restaurant! Suddenly everyone but the two of us disappeared. The waitresses, waiters, the maitre d' and the people all vanished right before our very eyes. Dennis and I were completely alone in this huge amazing restaurant. We looked about in staunch amazement, wondering where everyone had gone. Did they leave or did we? How could a whole restaurant full of people just disappear?

In one breath, Dennis asked, "Where is everyone? How can all these people just vanish? Are we in a time warp or what?"

"I believe, Dennis, we may have been shifted into another dimension," I exclaimed.

"If so, then how could the building go with us? If we took the restaurant, then where do you think all those people are? Did we move or did they?"

As we sat in absolute amazement, the music seemed to surround us, so soft and serene ... so out of this world!

What else could it be but Heaven? One would think we had been shifted to another planet, except it looked exactly like the restaurant; but everything took on a certain glow and a feeling of euphoria we had not experienced before. I will never forget that feeling. It was not anything I had ever felt before except for the time I died and really was in Heaven.

We wanted for nothing; we were so completely content. What could one want or need when you had it all? We prayed in the silence, "Please God don't let anything change! Just let it last forever!"

The peace and serenity seemed to stretch into infinity. We spoke in whispers, afraid we might upset the delicate balance. Heaven can't be any better than this!

I had read that there are duplicate worlds, the visible and the invisible. I tried to explain to Dennis, "Everything is exactly the same except that it is all so much more ecstatic, that magical other-worldly feeling and the absence of all the people. This must be the duplicate of our own world, but if so, how can it be so much more euphoric? We are told that there is a duplicate of all universes and all the planets. Perhaps we have somehow been transported into that other dimension."

We had never known such bliss! The beauty filled our souls and we hoped it would last forever. "If I am dreaming, I hope I never wake up!" Dennis exclaimed.

We have no idea how long this euphoria lasted. Was it a minute, a week, or a year? Time was of no consequence. We had it all. Nothing else mattered in the least except our prayer, "Please, God, don't let it end."

But then as suddenly as it had come, the ecstasy was gone, and we were back in the same environment as when we came in: people chatting, waiters, waitresses and the maitre d' in full swing. All this seemed so ordinary compared to what we just experienced. It looked the same except it had lost its magic, that "other world" feeling.

We ordered dinner. Though we were famished when we came in, food no longer had any appeal. After this experience, we both knew we could never be the same. We ate in silence as if trying to bring back the magic. Whatever caused this shift in dimensions or whatever it was, I hope to have the privilege of experiencing it again. If this utopia is a small sample of heaven, how could anyone fear death! The strange thing about all this was that none of the people in the restaurant knew anything out of the ordinary had happened!

If Dennis and I had tried to tell them about what we had just experienced, do you think they would believe us? You know they would not. In most cases if we don't experience it ourselves, we become a "Doubting Thomas."

Remember when the other disciples tried to tell Thomas that Jesus had actually returned from the dead and had visited them during Thomas' absence?

"Doubting Thomas" openly said he would not believe unless he could put his finger in the wound in Jesus' side. So when the Master suddenly appeared to the disciples again, Jesus told Thomas to thrust his hand into the wound in His side. Remember what Thomas said, "Oh, my Lord and my God!" That surely made a believer of Thomas!

It would take something extraordinary to convince most people that there are such things as Miracles, Angels and heavenly experiences. But I have to wonder if I had never experienced such things, would I believe?

Once while wide awake—and I was not alone nor was I the only one who experienced it—we were shifted into another dimension, and what was most bizarre about it was, the two of us, among hundreds of other people, all in the same location, were the only two who experienced it.

We do not have the slightest idea of how much time had passed.

It is a scientific fact that the second-hand on a watch will show a different amount of time that passes in a given period of time depending on who is wearing the watch. I have even had the experience of time standing still more than once.

Time really is flexible. One must experience this phenomenon to understand or even believe it.

Who can understand the grandeur of dying unless they have experienced it? In my own case and numerous others, after a near-death experience (NDE), life takes on a whole new perspective. After such an encounter, one takes on a heightened awareness and a sacredness of life, and yet there is no fear of dying. Things like career, money and ego have much less prominence in our lives.

Quantum physics is showing us that solid objects are not really solid. Deepak Chopra tells us that our bodies are 99.999 percent space. Things are not always what they seem to be. My husband, Lou, and I were discussing how this fits in with knowing our own power. God gave the power over all creation to man.

We wanted to light a bayberry candle to commemorate the New Year. Picking up a candle that obviously was not bayberry fragrance, I said, "We will decree this candle to be bayberry, and since it is an inanimate thing, it has no power to deny it."

Carrying this thesis a little further, we must remember God did not put all He had created under the body's control. He put man (who is spirit) in charge of all his creation. So, we can say to the body, "I decree that you shall, as of two PM tomorrow be ten years younger in every desirable way."

And the body has no power to deny our command. The scripture backs me up when it says, "Thou shalt decree a thing and it shall be established unto you."

Jesus made the same admonition when He said that anything you ask in faith, believing, shall be yours. He made it clear that this is true if you do not doubt. He went on to declare that you could say to a mountain, "Be thou cast into the midst of the sea and it shall be done."

Again we are talking of inanimate objects. If we decree something concerning another human being, remember that other person has the right to deny it whereas an inanimate object does not. This is why I like to do healing for others without their knowledge. This way they can't use their negative power to doubt or refuse the healing or possibly affect it negatively. If the person for whom you have done a healing is not healed, do not be discouraged. A healing is never wasted. That healing will manifest somewhere, possibly in a place you had neither one thought of. And if that person has some reason to reject the healing, that is his right. It is really up to God anyway.

All of this figures in becoming "prosperity conscious." In her book *You Own the Power,* Rosemary Altea tells us how to anchor this power wherever we wish. Her instructions go something like this: Consider the Chakras.

We know they are power vortexes in the body and we have other areas where we can feel the power. I followed her instructions and it works. Try this:

Center all your attention on the palm of each of your hands. With your middle finger draw a circle in the palm of your left hand. You will have a strong sensation there, like itching, pressure, heat or a tickling sensation. After you have done this to each hand, sit quietly and send all your thought to this area.

I did this and I began to feel a power in my hands, much like the sensation I get when I do a healing for someone. Knowing that blue is for healing and comes from Lord Michael, I began to visualize a blue ball of energy between my hands. The sensation was powerful. So I put my hands on different parts of my body that I felt could use a healing and it really worked.

Another powerful technique I want to share with you that I have used. Plant a seed in someone's future. I did this again yesterday for a dear friend. I wrote a check and told her that I was planting this seed to bring about prosperity into her life. I have no doubt that she will see the effects very soon.

I want to share this true story with you.

PLANT A SEED

A dear friend was down on her luck which was why God sent her to me. After some time, she was still complaining that she couldn't find the kind of job she wanted and she was in debt and badly in need of money. I said to her, "I refuse to tolerate these problems you are having. I want it stopped as of right now!"

I reached for my checkbook and wrote her a check, saying, "I am planting this seed for you to get the job you want, at the salary that will make you happy; for you to get out of debt and have the money you need from now on."

She protested, "I can't even pay you for my counseling. How can I accept money from you?"

I said, "That is what makes this seed so powerful. It is not my money. It is my tithe which makes it God's money, so you cannot refuse it or you would be throwing God's gift back in his face."

She smiled and said, "That is sneaky, you know."

I laughed, "Yes, I know! Ain't it great?"

The interesting thing is that within two weeks she landed the job she wanted at the salary she desired and within two months she was out of debt. She hasn't had a money problem since.

If I may reiterate, when you don't know at present if you have a dollar in your pocket or not, like the millionaires I have known, you have achieved that illusive state of prosperity consciousness. And so to sum it all up, what does it mean to be prosperity conscious? According to Webster's dictionary it means to succeed, thrive, have good fortune, to be and feel wealthy. And consciousness means to be conscious of that feeling, a knowing that all is well. As you can see "Prosperity Consciousness" is indeed a journey into an over-all philosophy of living. It truly is a "Magnificent Journey."

About the Author

Audrey Craft Davis is a published author, writer, lecturer, entrepreneur, and a veteran teacher and counselor. She has earned doctorate degrees in Divinity, Psychology and Metaphysics. She is included in *Who's Who of American Women* and *Who's Who in American Education* as well as the Register of Honors, *Dictionary of International Biography* of Cambridge, England.

Audrey is known for her work in radio and TV. You can find her other books and information listed at the end of this book along with where and how they can be purchased. Her books have kept her busy with book signings, seminars, workshops and classes. She also writes for several magazines.

Her books on practical metaphysics are featured in many other countries as far removed as The Luminous Wisdom Foundation, Ghana, West Africa and The Radiant Light Centre Library of Nigeria. Her book, *Metaphysical Techniques That Really Work* (Blue Dolphin, 2004), was featured at amazon.com for six weeks and rated five-star.

Audrey lives in Oldsmar, Florida and has a grown son and daughter. Her dear husband, Lou, passed away in 2002.

Metaphysical Techniques That Really Work

Audrey Craft Davis

ISBN: 1-57733-128-1, 148 pp., 5.5 x 8.5, paper, $14.95

Metaphysical Techniques That Really Work will guide you in the unfolding of your higher spiritual and mental potentials. Author Audrey Craft Davis describes the techniques and offers true stories from her personal experience. Next, she guides you with step-by-step instructions on how to use the technique and incorporate it into your life. With a little practice you'll learn to do the following:

- **Initiate contact** with your unseen guidance and earthbound spirits.
- **Bi-location** - projection techniques that allow your astral body to be seen in a different location.
- **Energy boosting** that will last for hours.
- **Numerology** - a short course in the magic of numbers and how to use them to your advantage.
- **The law of prosperity** - harvest the abundance that is your spiritual right.
- **Storing subtle energy** for later use with levitation, psychometry, healing and astral projection.
- **Do-it-yourself past-life regression** - a simple technique requiring no hypnosis.
- **Communicate with the spirits of departed loved ones** - several techniques.
- **Instant alpha trance** with a "Cyber-Optic" visual.
- **Aura reading** - the electromagnetic field can reveal more than you know.
- **Ultra-powerful healing techniques** that really work.
- **Much, much more!**

Metaphysical Encounters of a Fourth Kind

An Exacting Science

Audrey Craft Davis

ISBN: 978-1-57733-204-6, 144 pp., 5.5 x 8.5, paper, $14.95

Apply Metaphysical principles to every area of your life. Learn Treasure-Mapping and Cyber-optic viewing.

Your thoughts are powerful. If you think your world stinks, it does, but if you think it is lined with rainbows, it is. Change your thought; change your world.

Do you know that love is the greatest force in the world? Wrap yourself and your loved ones in the magic of love.

All of this and more is contained in this book, and it shows how metaphysics can be an exacting and practical science.

Making Love with God

The Art of Mental Connection

Audrey Craft Davis

ISBN: 978-1-57733-191-5, 132 pp., 5.5 x 8.5, paper, $14.95

When I met Lou, his doctors had informed him that he had three months to live. We stretched those three months to twenty-three years of sheer joy and happiness. We traveled all over the world and took 78 wonderful cruises.

This book is about literally bringing God into your love life. God gave me this plan because I was concerned about my husband's heart every time we made love. This book is for all couples, and even for those who are seeking companionship. Begin with God at the helm and the relationship will blossom.

Printed in the United States
95050LV00002B/9/A

9 781577 332039